THE
INNER GAME
OF
FINGERSTYLE GUITAR

HOW TO
BLEND YOUR INTUITION, INTELLECT, AND EMOTIONS TO ACHIEVE GUITAR MASTERY

ADAM RAFFERTY

To request permissions, contact the publisher at office@adamrafferty.com

Paperback: ISBN 978-1-7345755-0-7
Audiobook: ISBN 978-1-7345755-1-4
E-book: ISBN 978-1-7345755-2-1
Kindle Book: ISBN 978-1-7345755-3-8

First paperback edition January 2020.

Cover art by Damonza.com
Layout by Damonza.com

Printed by Amazon KDP in the USA.

Crescent Ridge Publishing, LLC
323 Pipe Stave Hollow Road
Miller Place, NY 11764

adamrafferty.com

As a thank you for purchasing this book, I'd like to offer you some free online resources, which you can access by visiting or clicking on the link below.

Enjoy this good stuff!

http://adamrafferty.com/inner-game-book-free-gift

For Mike Longo

*Thank you for having taken me
on as your musical apprentice.*

*I cherish your profound teachings, your wisdom,
your humanity, and your humor every single day.*

Contents

Introduction

Congratulations on taking this next incredible step in your musical journey! The fact that this book is in your hands is no accident. You attracted it because you are ready for it.

You found this book, and it found you.

It is my hope that in the pages ahead you will find the perfect message to help take your musical and personal development to the next level. I will offer you my best ideas, guidance, life stories, and techniques to help improve your inner game and apply it to your music.

What is the 'inner game'?

The inner game is the game of understanding yourself. It's everything other than the raw guitar information that you'd find in a textbook.

The inner game is the game of mastering your ego, emotions, cultivating your intellect, your craft, confronting boredom, frustration, developing discipline, and allowing things to unfold naturally.

When you become serious about any art, you start playing

an inner game. Whether you're learning to play guitar, paint with watercolor, or anything else, the urge to improve can churn up feelings of frustration, confusion, and maybe even despair.

That's actually the ego at work. You feel this separate little "me" in the fight to improve yourself. Navigating through this maze, getting your ego out of the way, and allowing your art to flourish is all part of the inner game.

So mastering your art is actually a way of mastering yourself.

Is this book for you?

Can you answer "yes" to any of the following?

- Your soul lights up when you play music, but you feel confused about what to learn or practice next.

- You feel that your musical instinct is right, but you're not sure about how to improve your technique, theory, and rhythm.

- You've read about things like modes, chord inversions, and theory but the ideas never stick or integrate with your playing.

- You have limited practice time.

- You experience self-doubt and nervousness when you perform in front of others, even though you can play perfectly at home.

- You are currently self-taught.

- You feel you are stuck in a rut, playing the same old stuff.

- You follow online lessons and have piles of DVD's and

books but can't get momentum and a thread of learning started. It always feels like starting from square one.

If you answered "yes" to any of these questions, then this book is for you.

You are not alone. Years ago I was as lost and confused as you may be on every single point mentioned.

I can remember my dizzy days as a young music student. I'd be bewildered by random bits of information from guitar magazines. My practicing would jump from one idea to another, and I'd feel hopeless with big musical projects.

I'd attend concerts and see the enormous gap between where I was and where the seasoned pros were. And if I ever had to play solo guitar, I'd get unbearably nervous, almost to the point of vomiting.

Like you, I knew I had music in me, but I lacked a plan. I desperately needed a system to understand how my music, mind, and soul ticked.

When the student is ready, the teacher appears

When I couldn't take these unanswered questions any longer, my mentor appeared, as if from nowhere.

And now this book is in your hands because you are ready for this information.

Imagine the future musical you

For the next minute, I'd like you time-travel, and imagine the future musical you:

- You see yourself fully understanding the music you are playing, and you enjoy your delicious knowledge.

- You easily understand harmony and theory.

- You're practicing effectively, and enjoyably getting results.

- Your groove is impeccable.

- You're performing in front of others confidently with a smile on your face, and they are enjoying your music.

- You understand the blend of your emotions, intellect, and intuition as you play.

- The music is playing itself—through you.

Allow that vision to sink in for about sixty seconds. If you hold that vision, and continually come back to it, you will surely achieve it.

Who am I and why should you listen to me?

My name is Adam Rafferty, and I'm a guitarist, composer, and teacher. I started playing guitar at age five and just turned fifty! (OMG, how did that happen?) So that's forty-five years of music study and playing, thirty years of teaching, and I am *still learning something new about music, guitar, and life every day.*

As a teen I had my first big challenge studying classical guitar. Following that, I played jazz guitar in New York City through my twenties and thirties. I still think of myself as a jazz player even though I've been playing mainly solo fingerstyle guitar for the last twelve years.

It was during my jazz-guitar period that I met my mentor,

a world-class jazz pianist, composer, and arranger. He gave me musical and personal training of the highest order.

It was an intense master-apprentice relationship. Our minds melded. Many of my vague ideas became clear and precise simply through being around him.

Even though he was officially "just a music teacher," our lessons went far beyond music. Music was simply the vehicle through which a deeper teaching was conveyed.

The concepts I will teach you started as lessons from him, but have since taken hold in my life as real experiences, which I now own. If I were merely "teaching the teaching" to you, the words would be hollow and convey nothing. That's why everything I will tell you here is backed up by my own (sometimes painful) life experience. I have paid the full price of admission for any advice I will give you.

Using the concepts in this book, I have accomplished things far beyond what I dreamed would ever be possible.

For example, I have gotten to play thousands of guitar concerts and festivals all over the world in Germany, Austria, Italy, Bermuda, Russia, Kazakhstan, Singapore, USA, Scotland, England, Estonia, Finland, and Poland, to name a few. I've received twenty-million video views on YouTube, released ten CD's, built a DVD instructional series, and built a successful and lively online guitar school. And most of all, I've enjoyed my musical life tremendously.

I'm not saying this to brag or show off. I'm saying it to inspire you, because you can do it, too. My achievements became possible because I learned certain principles, which I will now share with you.

What will you learn?

Some of the ideas you'll learn will be musical, designed to help clear up any misunderstandings you may have. No music reading is required, but we will address musical ideas.

Many more ideas will be related to the psycho-spiritual inner game of learning, improving, and mastering yourself, your productivity, and your practice.

It gives me great joy to pass this knowledge on to you and help you discover new dimensions within yourself.

Soon you'll be able to see your way on the path more clearly, and watch in amazement as your practicing, playing, and life improve in leaps and bounds.

Thanks for inviting me to join you on this part of your journey.

Let's get started.

PART ONE

YOUR SOUL

Chapter One

Your Instinct Is Perfect

"Have the courage to follow your heart and intuition. They somehow already know what you truly want to become. Everything else is secondary."

~ Steve Jobs

AT MY FIRST lesson with my mentor, I told him, "Well, I play a little guitar, but I'm actually interested in piano and jazz theory." I had played guitar my whole life but was uninspired to study jazz guitar and wanted to learn piano.

After I fumbled for three weeks through beginner jazz voicings on the piano, my mentor slyly said, "You said you play guitar, right? Bring your guitar in next week. I'd like to hear what you do."

At that next lesson, he picked up his African hand drum and told me to simply play some funk/blues guitar in Bb along with him so he could hear me play.

As I closed my eyes and dug into playing with him, I was pretty scared and didn't know what to think. I knew I couldn't impress this guy with chops or showing off. He'd played with Dizzy Gillespie and had seen and heard it all, so I just had to do what I did best, which was groove and play the blues.

Essentially, all I could show him was my instinct.

To my surprise, when we finished, he was glowing.

"Man that was groovin'!" he said. "If you keep playing like that, you're going to get all the record dates!" (That's New York jazz-guy slang for "recording sessions.")

I felt shocked, delighted, and validated. It was like an initiation. Even though I originally felt I wanted to learn piano, in that instant I realized that what I really wanted was an apprenticeship with a jazz master, so I trusted his rerouting me back to the guitar.

He acknowledged my basic talent, and saw that the guitar was a part of me much more than the piano was. For the next seventeen years he taught me harmony, melody, rhythm, improvisation, composition, and counterpoint.

That was the day he took me under his wing and I became his apprentice. The journey began.

Looking back, I can see that there was a thread that ran through all my studies with him. It was this: whenever I strayed from my musical instinct by getting lost in intellect or ego, he'd pull me back... reminding me that "musical instinct is perfect."

It took a while to understand the depth and profundity of that statement, but as I develop and mature, the truth of it rings clearer and clearer.

'Be not the doer'

When you experience musical perfection, you are actually allowing a natural behavior of divine physics to play out through you. Perfection comes through you on its own, and you don't feel like the "doer" of it.

It feels awesome, and I am sure you have felt it. I want you to experience this instinctual perfection more and more as you make music.

Of course, you must learn and practice the mechanics and techniques of proper music making. But the tools by themselves don't make the music. *You* make the music, and you use the tools required to do the job.

Feeling musical truth in your body

My mentor would often give me late-night music lessons by singing phrases to me over the telephone. When he sung these, it often would touch me so deeply that I'd feel the truth of it as a tickle sensation in my solar plexus.

I would find myself giggling from inside after he'd sing the phrases, and all I could do was surrender and think to myself, "Wow, that's the musical truth, and this guy knows the truth." It was an amazing feeling of total honesty.

I also started noticing, in other areas of life, that when I would shed a little layer of ego and be honest with myself, I always got that same little tickle in the stomach.

I'm sure you've felt the feeling of musical truth in your body. Maybe you've felt joy when dancing to a groove, or felt your heart open up when a beautiful melody was played. It feels like a big "yes."

What's important is that you must stay honest and tuned in to your truth.

How can you know your musical truth from falsehood?

You'll know the music you are playing is true if:

- It feels right and lights you up inside
- You are allowing it to unfold
- Your body and muscles feel strong as you do it
- It feels like it has a life of its own
- It feels like "yes"

Conversely, you'll know something you are playing is false if:

- You're coming from a place of force or effort
- You can't sing it back easily
- Your muscles go weak, (you can't foot-tap, snap your fingers, or dance to it)
- It centers around the idea of "the little me" doing it
- A small, quiet voice inside says "no"

For further philosophical reading, I highly recommend the books *Power vs. Force* and *Truth vs. Falsehood*, by David Hawkins. You can apply everything he says there to music.

There is a wonderful quote from psychiatrist and hypnotherapist Brian Weiss that pretty much sums up the learning-and-intuition balancing act:

"Come from the heart, the true heart, not the head. When in doubt, choose the heart. This does not mean to deny your own experiences and that which you have empirically learned through the years. It means to trust yourself to integrate intuition and experience. There is a balance, a harmony to be nurtured, between the head and the heart. When the intuition rings clear and true, loving impulses are favored."

The takeaway

Learning new musical skills, concepts, and techniques is something you will do for the rest of your life. It's necessary for your development, and yes, it does require intellect, study, and practice. That's the homework.

Doing your homework will help you widen your palette of colors, see new possibilities, make new musical connections, listen better, understand more, and come up with new, creative solutions.

However, when it's time to engage in music making, you must trust in the skills and concepts you've developed and then forget them. You must have the courage to surrender the intellect and go into instinct mode as you make music.

Listen to your deepest musical intuition, feel your heart and body in connection with your head, and allow a perfect musical instinct to guide you.

Chapter Two

Focus on Your Strengths

"Every superhero has a unique superpower that gives them an advantage. In other words, it's okay to diversify your skills, but do not hesitate to 'fully' capitalize on your strengths."

~ Izey Victoria Odiase

ALLOW ME TO ask you a question.

What music lights up your soul?

It may seem silly to ask this question. You may be thinking, "I know what I like, so why should I bother reading this?"

Well, there are some dead-end streets ahead of you on the journey to becoming a better guitar player. I'd like to help you avoid them, saving you time, effort, and hardship.

Honesty with yourself about your musical loves and trusting your gut will make your journey easier.

It's not always easy though, and here's why.

As you learn, you will be exposed to many ideas and many styles of music. You may then start to reconsider things and even question yourself.

Some music will really touch you, and some won't. You may even appreciate how well someone plays, even if it's not your favorite style.

With the exposure to new information, it's easy to get confused and taken off your center. How can you be sure you are staying on course?

Start with your 'why'

A common piece of business advice is not to start with how you can do something but with why you are doing it. The why comes before the how.

The same applies to music.

When you take actions that support a love or a why, you'll have a lot more inspiration, patience, and creativity behind your work.

In music, your why is nonverbal. You can't say why you love music, but you feel it. That love will be your strength and fuel your inner genius to come up with incredible, creative solutions.

Allow me to give you two examples of how this follow-your-strengths axiom has played out for me. One example is positive, the other negative.

Success story: discovering the groove to 'Superstition'

I have loved the Stevie Wonder song "Superstition" since I was a kid. When I started my solo guitar journey, I thought, "Wow, that would be a cool tune to play!" Every time I'd hear it, I just wanted to dance. *Funkay!*

The key word here is "love." That was my why.

So I rolled up my sleeves and got to work on the arrangement. At first I could play the notes, yet I still hadn't cracked the secret to the groove and the feel.

Because of my love for that tune, I was able to tirelessly dig, dig, dig, deeply and patiently, for months. Eventually the percussive solution revealed itself, appearing like an unexpected blossom in springtime!

Key point: it didn't feel like "I" did it. It felt like *the music revealed itself.* That's the telltale sign of it *not* being an ego-based solution.

And now a guitar fail, as promised!

I've made mistakes too. Here's one.

After playing at many festivals and seeing incredible players, I thought to myself, "Geez, I've played for forty-plus years. *I should* be able to play the thumb-pick/boom-chick style."

I also admired how well others could do it. (That's not a deep enough place to come from.) I loved how much they love what they do.

So I set out for months of discipline practicing Chet Atkins-style thumb-picking, yet it never clicked. Why not?

The more it didn't click, the more frustrated I got with myself. How could I be such a moron that I couldn't figure this out? My ego took a beating! I was really down on myself.

But... when I got really honest, I realized: *I never listened to that music in my life, hadn't grown up with it, and would never sing songs in that style to myself as I walked down the street.*

I didn't really dig country music, but felt I *should.*

The mistakes made?

- I was focused on "how." I wasn't focused on a "love."

- I was focused on "me" (ego) and "my ability"—not on a love of music.

- I didn't stay with my strengths.

- I wasted tremendous amounts of time and effort.

In essence, this was the ego at work.

And if you are a disciplined person like me, it's easy to get disciplined with *the wrong thing* like I did. That's one of the dead-ends I mentioned earlier. This is why I advise you to be very clear with yourself on your loves and your whys—*first.*

You are not a computer

Another model that's inaccurate is the "mind as computer" model.

In our Western education system, we are taught that the mind is like an empty hard drive where a program can simply be installed at will.

It's dangerous to learn music this way, and here's why.

You can hear many young, classical music students who

have learned through this philosophy. In the end they all sound the same, and often sound quite cold, even if they are technically correct.

It's zombie-esque, as if there is no personality in the music.

So don't think that you are a computer that can spit back anything. Listen to your heart as you learn.

Don't 'should' all over yourself

Sometimes we think we *should* like something for some reason (usually social pressure and conformity, even if we don't realize it).

For example:

- You *should* like jazz, but it hasn't really grabbed you personally.

- You *should* like classical music, but it just isn't hitting you.

- You *should* like old bluegrass because everyone likes it, but you don't like it.

Forget about all this. If you feel you "should" love something, *you don't love it.*

Good vibrations

Here's a great example of someone who is very honest about his musical loves.

When I was in college I had a composition teacher by the name of Anthony Newman.

He is a keyboard genius unlike any I've ever seen. I remember him coming into class at 8 am, looking like he just rolled out of bed, and sitting on the piano bench in cross-legged, full-lotus position, like a Buddhist monk.

With no warm up, he'd play passages from the "Goldberg Variations," by Bach, with the most insanely virtuosic keyboard technique I'd ever heard or seen. He simply tossed it off, as if it were a mundane task like taking out the garbage.

After class, we once chatted, and I made an apologetic comment, saying, "Well, I know you think jazz is stupid, but I really love it."

He interrupted me immediately.

"No. I don't think jazz is stupid at all. It simply does not *vibrate* with me."

Those words struck me like a bolt of lightning. He was absolutely clear about acknowledging the *validity* of a different musical style, but also clear on what "vibrated" with him and what didn't.

He made no judgement about the style; he simply took full responsibility for what he liked or didn't like.

What do you vibrate with (musically, of course)?

Let's do a little detective work.

What was your earliest musical inspiration? Was it the radio? Was it your parents' record collection? Was it singing in music class or church?

When you are in the car and flipping through the stations, occasionally you will stumble upon a tune that really gets you.

It makes you turn the volume up and act silly—grooving along, maybe even singing out loud.

It's critical to be honest with yourself about the music you enjoy…

- Even if it would be embarrassing to others
- Even if it's not "cool"
- Even if your partner or friends don't like it

A written exercise—do this now!

I'd like you to do the following exercise.

It's designed to make you look inward and get in touch with your why. It will take two minutes.

Grab a paper and pen and jot down the answers so you can look back at them later. (Don't use a smartphone. Please write on paper.)

1. List your ten favorite musical artists. The first five will be easy, but then for six to ten, you'll need to stretch.
2. What are your five all-time favorite albums or CD's?
3. Has a piece of music ever brought you to tears? If so, which one?
4. Was there ever a tune you listened to over and over and over again?
5. List five musical styles that don't touch you emotionally or you absolutely don't like.
6. List five musical styles you think you *should* like but haven't gotten around to listening to.
7. Who is your partner's favorite musical artist? How

would you secretly rate that artist on a scale of one to ten (ten being best)?

8. Who were your parents' favorite musical artists? How would you secretly rate those artists on a scale of one to ten?

9. Does your best friend like your favorite music?

10. Does your partner like the music you like?

The takeaway

Focus on your strengths, not your weaknesses. This will allow your inner genius to shine forth.

What you loved musically as a kid and teenager is a good indication of your musical vibration. Stay with your musical loves, and you'll be happy and joyful as you do your musical homework.

Solutions will appear as if by magic when your entire heart and soul are engaged in the process.

The degree of self-honesty you possess will speed up your process and make your musical journey easier.

Don't waste your precious time and effort on music you think you "should" like because of any kind of social pressure, or to get approval from anyone.

Once you are in alignment with that which you truly love, you'll be in the perfect position to create a plan and achieve your greatest musical goals.

Chapter Three

Manifesting Your Musical Vision

"The real magic is in making the intangible idea, the creative impulse, manifest and live in our reality."

~ Mark Ryan

RIGHT NOW I'M going to ask you to think of yourself as the guitar version of "the karate kid."

In the movie *The Karate Kid*, the young Daniel goes to study karate with Mr. Myagi, the master.

Instead of karate, Mr. Myagi has him do a number of housecleaning and maintenance activities that seem to have no relation to martial arts training.

Mr. Myagi assigns Daniel the following housework:

- Wax on, wax off (waxing his car)
- Sanding the floor

- Painting the fence

For each task, Mr. Myagi shows exactly the circular hand movements, along with special breathing.

Daniel works into the dark hours of the night waxing Mr. Myagi's car, and Mr. Myagi even comes out in the dark, to correct Daniel's technique.

Daniel loses faith in his teacher. His anger builds as he feels he is being taken advantage of to do housework, being strung along with the false hope of getting karate lessons. He finally explodes at Mr. Myagi and tells him how he feels.

Mr. Myagi firmly calls Daniel over, once again reviewing the three hand movements used for the housework. Next, he calmly says, "Show me 'wax on, wax off'," and in an unexpected flash, he yells, "Hi-yaaaa" and tries to strike Daniel.

To Daniel's amazement, he defends against Mr. Myagi's blow with the hand motion he practiced from "wax on, wax off."

He then realizes he was being taught karate the entire time.

This chapter is similar. You have to be like the karate kid. (Too bad I can't get you to clean my house, though!)

The craft and techniques you will learn next may not feel like music. Even if they seem unrelated, I promise you they will help you manage your mind, set goals, and bring ideas into the material world. And those skills are essential for you as a musician.

The secret

I'm going to tell you a secret. Here it is all at once.

You are a divine creator, and every single word you say,

vision you have, and act you perform, magically brings forth the creations and situations you experience into your life.

That's called *manifestation*. You already do it all the time.

And now that I've given you the whole shebang, it probably sounds too intense, unbelievable, and woo-woo New Age-y.

So let's backtrack and start with a simple illustration.

Cosmic coffee

Maybe you start your day with a cup of coffee. It seems to you like no big deal. You've been doing that for years.

Let's look at the mechanics though…

1. You start with an image in your mind of a cup of coffee.

2. You find your way through whatever actions are necessary to get that coffee. Maybe you make it, maybe you go to a Starbucks… whatever.

3. You have a cup of coffee in your hands.

Now let's eliminate Step Two so you can see it play out like a magic act.

•   You start with an image in your mind of a cup of coffee.

•   You have a cup of coffee in your hands.

When you see it like this, you can conclude that the vision of the coffee is the seed you plant in the mind, and the actual cup of coffee is the flowering and manifestation of the idea. (We'll address Step Two later on.)

Manifesting unwanted things

Brian Tracy, the motivational speaker and author, warns: "Never say anything about yourself you do not want to come true."

The mind does not care if you plant a positive seed or a negative one. Its job is to bring forth the flowering of the seed you plant.

If you had a backyard garden, you could plant roses, or you could plant nightshade, which is a highly poisonous plant. The ground itself does not care. It simply produces what you intended to grow.

So it's important to guard your thoughts and think only of what you do want.

(That's one more reason to guard your mental input—especially social media.)

The importance of setting goals

A person of average talent and intelligence who sets specific goals and chips away at them will become much more successful than a super-talented genius with no goals.

When a person has no goals, they tend to wander from one thing to the next aimlessly, doing whatever feels good in the moment, with no sense of direction. They flounder and start something new every day, based on whim. They'll never know if they've reached a goal because they were never aiming at anything in the first place.

Imagine getting in your car and driving with no destination in mind. It might be an enjoyable activity for a little while. You take every turn and backroad you feel like, but eventually you wonder, "Where am I going?"

When will you arrive at your destination? Never, because you don't have one in mind in the first place.

That's okay for an afternoon drive, because your goal might be the process of having a relaxed day and going where life takes you. But do you want the rest of your life to be like that?

Setting your first goal

The first step in achievement is to set a specific goal.

Goals can be small or big. Size does not matter. The simple act of setting a goal is a quantum leap in the direction of achieving what you want.

The most effective goals are:

- Specific
- Measurable
- Time-bound

So let's say your goal is to practice guitar more. A vague and undefined version of the goal would be:

- I want to practice guitar more.

Okay, that's a start, but we can do better.

Let's get more *specific*. What will you practice?

- I want to practice *my version of "Yesterday" by the Beatles* more.

Can we make it *measurable*?

Without measuring, you'll have no sense of whether the goal is achieved or not.

- I will practice my version of *"Yesterday" by the Beatles for at least thirty minutes.*

Now, can we make it *time-bound to a deadline*? By when will you have done it?

- *This Wednesday at 7 pm, I will practice my version of "Yesterday" by the Beatles for at least thirty minutes.*

This is looking good. You've taken aim at a specific target, and you know when you will get down to work, and for how long.

Chunking down big goals

Sometimes a big goal can feel overwhelming. That means it needs to be "chunked down" into smaller sub-goals.

Big musical goals are things like:

- Performing a live set
- Recording a CD, a single, or a video
- Starting a band
- Learning a new piece of music

Let's pick the goal, "Recording my music on CD" and chunk it down into sub-goals.

(In a few years, CD's may be a thing of the past, as services such as Spotify may become the norm. Let's just use CD production for example purposes.)

Recording my music on CD:

- Pick the tunes

- Practice the tunes

- Decide whether to record at home or in a studio

- Get photos taken

- Find a CD designer

- Find a CD-pressing plant

- Pay for any cover-song licensing

- Send the music to radio stations

And of course each of these tasks would have to be chunked down even further.

There's still one problem, though. Certain sub-goal chunks may depend on the completion of other chunks.

In the CD example, you could do photos anytime. But you need to practice before you go to a recording studio, and you need to decide which tunes you will play before you practice.

So how can we determine the order in which to do each chunk?

Backwards goal-planning

An ingenious technique when there are several steps in a goal process is called *backwards planning*.

Here's how it works:

Write your final goal down at the top of a list, and step backwards through time. As you go down the list, each new item is the logical step of what *had to have happened immediately before*, until you find yourself at the present moment where you currently stand.

This may sound confusing, so here's a simple illustration.

Imagine you want to go swimming later on today. What are the steps from the future vision back to the present?

Future to present:

- Go swimming (future vision)
- Jump in the pool (happens immediately before)
- Put bathing suit on (happens immediately before)
- Travel to swimming pool (happens immediately before)
- Get in car (happens immediately before)
- Pack bathing suit in gym bag (present moment)

After completing the list of tasks (future to present), *flip the list upside down* and you'll have the perfect step-by-step list, always knowing exactly what to do next.

Present to future (flipped list):

- Pack bathing suit in gym bag (present moment)
- Get in car
- Travel to swimming pool
- Put bathing suit on
- Jump in the pool
- Go swimming (future vision)

Backwards goal-planning example: the dinner party

Let's do another example. Imagine that you'd like to throw a fabulous dinner party for friends and family. Let's start with the end result first and step backwards through time:

Future to present:

- Everyone is enjoying the dinner party! (future vision)
- Food is brought to the table.
- Guests arrive.
- You prepare the meal.
- You clean your house.
- You go shopping for ingredients and drinks.
- You decide on what dishes you will prepare.
- You invite guests.
- You decide on a good time and date for the party. (present moment)

Now it's time to flip the list upside down so you have a step-by-step list, always showing you what to do next:

Present to future (flipped list):

- You decide on a good time and date for the party. (present moment)
- You invite guests.
- You decide on what dishes you will prepare.
- You go shopping for ingredients and drinks.
- You clean your house.
- You prepare the meal.
- Guests arrive.
- Food is brought to the table.
- Everyone is enjoying the dinner party! (future vision)

You can use the backwards-planning technique for all kinds

of musical goals, such as laying out a practice plan, preparing for a show, a recording—or even just preparing a single piece of music.

What if you can't figure out all the steps?

Remember our "cosmic coffee" story at the beginning of the chapter? That example was meant to illustrate that when you visualize something, it will manifest outwardly.

Backwards goal-planning is a technique to help you figure out a step-by-step plan to get you from the vision to your goal.

But what can you do if you are simply stumped with regard to the middle steps? Maybe you have a final vision, but no idea what to do next.

Or maybe you are simply inspired and feeling your way. You have a dream and end in mind, but no idea how it will actually come into being.

Sometimes when you don't have the steps laid out for you, discouragement can set in. Here's what you need to know so you don't get discouraged.

How to use your Reticular Activation System

Your mind is a powerful goal-seeking mechanism.

You are constantly achieving small goals even if you don't realize you are. Now it's time to learn how to harness that power.

Your mind takes in millions of bits of information each second. Different studies give different numbers of bits, so I don't know if anyone can count them. For the sake of argument, let's say your mind takes in four-million bits of raw info per second.

If you were to consciously take in all that information, you'd probably go completely crazy and have to be admitted to a mental hospital. As a protection against insanity, and as an aid to survival, your mind has a natural filter to help you identify anything relevant to your goals and to discard the rest.

That's the job of your Reticular Activation System (RAS), a bunch of cells that are located in your brainstem. Once you have a goal in mind, your Reticular Activation System allows you to filter the forty-thousand bits that are relevant to *you* and discard the rest.

All you actually need is your end vision, pictured clearly in your mind, and your RAS will run automatically in the background twenty-four hours a day, seven days a week, until you achieve your vision. Even if you don't realize it consciously, you'll always be taking the right steps you need to be taking.

Examples of the RAS at work

- You are seeking a career change but not sure where to look. You attend a cocktail party, and above the chatter of a room full of people your ear catches a few words of a conversation. You are automatically led to exactly the right person to talk to regarding your future plans.

- You need a new car and have been thinking about getting a red Volkswagen Beetle. Suddenly, it appears that wherever you look, there are red Volkswagen Beetles.

- You and your partner are thinking about having children. It seems that everywhere you look you now see pregnant women and families with small children in baby strollers.

How to program the RAS

Every time you look at your present surroundings or situation and acknowledge it as real and concrete, you are actually taking it in and building a future out of your present.

Your mind will take what you see as the instruction and make it the future goal, and continually discard everything else.

Do you see how this can be a problematic cycle?

It's not that your present situation is an absolute reality; in fact it's quite fluid. But if you go through life unconsciously, you will re-create your present circumstances on a day-to-day basis.

So that's why you must do an "interrupt" and consciously program the mind with your future vision, even if it feels unrealistic or like a fantasy or impossible.

Imagine that you have a fifteen-year-old, beat-up car that you can't stand to drive or be seen with. Yet you drive it every day and accept the reality. One day leads to the next, and you accept as real that this car is a mark of your identity.

A fast way to interrupt your cycle and plant the seed for owning a new car would be to simply close your eyes and imagine driving that new car. Imagine every detail: the smell, color, the feel of a strong accelerator, the tight hugging of curves, and the fast braking.

Even better would be to visit a car dealership and take a new car for a test drive. Smell it, feel it, and enjoy it.

The seed will have then been planted, and surely life will

take you to a new car even if you don't know the exact steps involved in getting it.

Cognitive dissonance

Your mind will accept a picture as reality. The mind does not know the difference between a picture in the mind and a picture actually out there in the environment.

If your current life and surroundings don't match up with the picture planted in your mind, you experience what is called "cognitive dissonance."

Cognitive dissonance is what happens when you experience a conflict between the inner picture and the outer picture.

Your mind will then seek to reorganize the outer picture or circumstances to match the inner picture as swiftly as possible.

How to use a vision board

Here's a technique I have used, and still use. You can wield enormous power with this, so use it wisely.

You can make what is called a vision board. You can either get a cork-style, pin-up board and tacks at your local office-supply store, or you can do it in a computer program such as Pixelmator or Photoshop.

(I suggest the old fashioned, hands on, tactile approach and always am in favor of stepping away from a computer, which has thousands of possible distractions and interruptions.)

Start looking through magazines, and cut out pictures which represent your ultimate dreams in any area of life. (I promise to show you how to do this for guitar playing and music, so just hang in there!)

Important: the pictures should represent these things as *already achieved.*

You may think that's a tad make-believe, but if you treat your goals as off in the future, that's where they'll stay: *always off in your future*, like a donkey with a carrot on a stick that it can never reach.

Pictures on your vision board may represent anything you desire to be, have, or experience. Here are some examples:

- A new living location

- You performing a new skill

- You playing guitar (this is a great image to keep in mind!)

- A financial statement with a huge net worth (you can scan a bank statement and add some zeros!)

- Any object you'd like to attract into your life (car, guitar)

- Anything else you desire

If one of your goals is to have a happy relationship, you might find a picture of a happy couple and paste a photo of your own face over one of the images.

By looking at the pictures on your vision board over the course of days, weeks, or months, you'll be planting just the seeds you need to initiate the interruption of your current circumstances.

My personal vision-board story

In 2006 I fell in love with the guitar playing of a guy named Tommy Emmanuel. His solo acoustic guitar gave me a new direction in my own playing. Even though I was already a pro jazz player in New York City at the time, a new inspiration took over my life.

Not only did I want to emulate Tommy's playing but I also wanted to perform with him. That was a dream of mine. I wasn't sure how to achieve it, as I was simply a fan with no real connection to him.

That year I went to a concert of his at B.B. King's blues club on 42nd street in New York City. I bought the ticket online, so on one side of the ticket was my name (the customer name), and on the other side was the show name.

It listed Tommy Emmanuel and his support act, Anthony Snape.

I decided to do some vision-board magic.

After the concert was over, I cut my name out of the one side of the ticket, and with scotch tape pasted it over the support act's name (sorry, Anthony!)

There was a huge gap between my present-moment reality and where I wanted to go. I could not yet do the backwards planning, as I had no idea what steps to take to get to my goal. So I turned it over to my subconscious.

The negative, self-doubting inner critic was saying things like:

- "Yeah, right. You're just dreaming!"
- "The vision-board stuff is stupid."

- "You'll never achieve that."

But I did it anyway, and looked at that ticket pinned up on my vision board, every day for a few years.

Voila!

The universe delivered!

In 2008 I got an email from a guy who had seen some of my YouTube videos.

"Would you be interested in opening for Tommy in Finland?" he asked.

Hell, yeah! And that led to being onstage with him in Bangkok, Frankfurt, Prague, Nashville, and other places I can't remember.

The biggest thrill of this process was to see the mind and universe in action. Getting the result was actually secondary, but still a thrill.

I saw that from starting with a vision, I was led each step of the way—perfectly, automatically, and unconsciously—toward exactly the goal I had in mind. This really brought tears to my eyes, and made my skin tingle and my back vibrate.

It wasn't just about getting a gig. It gave me the feeling that I had seen something much bigger about how the mind and universe operate.

In short: you decide the "what," so don't worry about the "how." Just let the universe take care of that part if you're unsure of the steps to take to get there.

The hidden power of writing out your goals

Writing your goals down is an extremely effective way to manifest them.

Here's why. The act of writing itself employs three modalities:

- Kinestheitc (you feel the pen or pencil)
- Visual (you see the words)
- Auditory (you hear yourself saying the words, even if they are silent)

When you use these three modalities together, your words will "wire" together and sink into the subconscious. Writing is extremely powerful in this regard.

Writing a proper goal statement

Here's what you must know to create an effective goal statement:

1. You must write the goal *as if it is already achieved*, or else it will always be in your future and never your present.

    Wrong: I want a Gibson Les Paul guitar.

    Right: I have a Gibson Les Paul guitar.

    Remember, you are programming your mind!

2. Involve positive emotion in the language.

    I find it hard to induce feelings artificially, so I start by allowing language to do it for me. Also, expressing gratitude takes it up a notch.

    Good: I have a Gibson Les Paul guitar.

Better: I am so happy and joyful to own a Gibson Les Paul guitar.

Even Better: I am so thankful to own my lovely Gibson Les Paul guitar.

3. Keep it simple and singular. Don't mix up too many ideas in one goal statement.

    Wrong: "I am so thankful to own this lovely Gibson Les Paul guitar, have a fun band, and also own a Marshall amp along with a Taylor acoustic guitar and a great home recording setup, and..."

    It's great to be thankful for this stuff, but if it's a goal you are trying to set up and plant mental seeds for, this will spread your mind too thin.

    Focus on one item per goal statement.

4. Take responsibility for yourself. Don't make your goal depend on the action, whim, or desire of someone else.

    Wrong: I am so happy and thankful that the club owner called me up to offer me a gig.

    Better: I am so happy and thankful to have a gig at a venue where my music is appreciated.

5. Don't put a limit on the goodness.

    Good: I am so happy and thankful to have a gig at a venue where my music is appreciated.

    Better: I am so happy and thankful to have multiple gigs at venues where my music is appreciated.

6. Adding a level of flow and ease is even better, as it will make you seek out the easiest way.

   Good: I am so happy and thankful to have multiple gigs at music venues where my music is appreciated.

   Better: I am so thankful that multiple offers for gigs flow to me easily and effortlessly.

(This may seem in conflict with Item Four, but here you are being receptive, whereas Item Four was an attempt to control someone.)

Write a description

Here's a close cousin of the goal-writing technique. You'll write a few paragraphs about what it is you desire, as if it is present and already in your life. Describe it in full detail on the level of your senses: sight, touch, sound, smell, taste (if it applies), and also emotionally.

Here's a true story about how this worked like magic in my life. I was in a phase where I found myself single and downright lonely. I had been on dates, but I couldn't seem to attract the right partner.

When I heard about this description-writing technique, I decided to write a full description of exactly the type of woman I wanted in my life. I clearly articulated the emotional and spiritual connection I desired, as well as the factors I find physically attractive.

The result? That exact person who I wrote about showed up in my life within a few months. She's my beloved partner and my best friend, and we live in a nice house with her son, a poodle, and two rabbits.

Try this, and I can almost guarantee you will get uncanny results.

Write an imaginary article or review about yourself

Could you write a glowing letter, article, or review about yourself from another person's point of view?

This is a cool, creative way of tricking your mind so you don't feel like you're being egotistical. It can get you into a flow of fantasy a little bit more easily. In writing, when you "channel" the voice of someone praising you, your subconscious will actually hear the praise and register it as if it's real (and it actually is!)

I have written glowing reviews for myself and then tucked them away for no one to see!

Make-believe posters or other visual items

If you have a goal that could involve a visual item like a tour poster, magazine cover, CD/album cover, or book cover, you can play pretend and let the imagination run wild. Just make a mock-up of the make-believe item.

The idea is to get your inner vision from a place of "I can't, I have doubts, how is it possible?" to "Wow, I already did it!" and allow for the cognitive dissonance in your mind to brew so that you get to where you want to go.

Visual item example #1: make-believe tour or gig poster

If you've never been on tour, maybe your dream is to tour as a musician. If so, why not make a tour poster?

That's right! Put your name and picture at the top, and list the cities of the imaginary tour. Allow your imagination to go wild. The entire world is your stage. Hang the poster up on your vision board. That's what I did.

Visual item example #2: book cover

Dreaming of writing your first book? You could either construct a make-believe book cover and put it on a real book you own, or download a book image from Google and use a graphics program to put your title and your own name on the cover.

Visual item example #3: magazine cover

Dreaming of being a mover and shaker in your chosen industry? Why not make a magazine cover of your industry's top magazine with you on the cover?

Visual items like these are not for ego inflation or to show around to others. They are for you alone. They will help you plant the seeds of accomplishment in your mind.

Result-oriented goals versus showing-up goals

On the one hand, I want to tell you: don't ever settle. Go for it.

However, as much as I don't want to say this, I will. Some

goals might be unrealistic. If you aim too high, too fast, or at something *completely* out of reach, you are setting yourself up for disappointment.

Here are some result-oriented goals that would probably be unrealistic for me:

- To be a world-class ballet dancer
- To be a world-class martial arts master
- To be an NBA basketball player

But I could set the following performance (or practice) goals:

- Go to a dance class twice a week
- Go to an aikido class twice a week
- Join a local basketball team

Results-orientation versus showing-up orientation in music

I get many students who learn about goal-setting and then say, "By next week, I plan to be able to play three Beatles guitar arrangements!" Whoa! If that doesn't happen, they'll be disappointed, discouraged, and cultivate a feeling that they failed.

I encourage them to set a showing-up goal instead. How about "practice thirty minutes a day"? From there, one can allow the results to show up on their own.

How big should the goal be?

You can have huge goals—that's no problem! Dream big!

But as you chunk down the goal into smaller, bite-sized tasks, it's good to set three possible levels:

- Minimum
- Target
- Outrageous

This three-step "MTO" idea is a technique I learned from a teacher named Raymond Aaron. It helps you avoid the disappointment you could feel with yourself if you bite off too much and don't reach your goal. Also, it helps you acknowledge your efforts so that you keep going.

For example, if you say "I will practice guitar six hours a day," you will probably fail, unless your lifestyle permits this (and it would not be good for your hands anyway!)

Set three levels of the goal. Here's an explanation of the three levels:

- *Minimum* – impossible to fail. You can finish this easily, no question. If you are under constraints, at least you know you did this and stayed in the game.

- *Target* – the sweet spot, what you really think you can do. Maybe there's just a little stretch here, but not much.

- *Outrageous* – you've gone above and beyond the target level. Pat yourself on the back. You've done good.

Real-life example:

Okay, I am writing this book now, but I have to keep my guitar playing in practice. Yesterday this was my practice goal, and I immediately made an MTO for myself.

- *Minimum* – Get guitar in my hands. That's all.

- *Target* – Play for thirty minutes, then I'm allowed to do other stuff. (That barely keeps me in the game, but on a writing day and busy work day, something is better than nothing.)

- *Outrageous* – Play for a few hours. (This is what I did. I had the guitar in my hands on and off until midnight.)

Had I told myself, "I'm playing guitar until midnight, no matter what!" I would have stressed myself with expectation and stressed my family by beating them off with a stick.

The MTO allowed me to ease in, stress-free, and take what came. I did have an eye on "outrageous," though.

The takeaway

The achievement of your musical goals is an outward manifestation of your inner picture.

It's critical to have goals. The mental picture of your goal is step one. The achieving of the goal is the sign that you have arrived at your destination.

Without goals, you have no idea if you've achieved what you want and may simply hop from one thing to another, or go in circles.

With the backwards-planning technique, you can plot the path to your goal by working backwards from the destination to where you now stand. Flip the list and you'll have a step-by-step plan.

And if you can't envision the steps, you can use your RAS (Reticular Activation System.) Create a clear picture of the goal in your mind, and simply allow your subconscious mind to guide you to your goal's achievement.

Your mind will magically ignore anything not relevant to

your goal, and clearly see that which will bring you closer to it. As the author Donald Hicks observed,

> "It's often been said that seeing is believing, but in many cases, the reverse is also true. Believing, results in seeing."

Now that you are getting your goals set up, let's get specific and take a look at the nuts and bolts of musical craft.

PART TWO

YOUR CRAFT

Chapter Four

Your Musical Studies

"Always two there are, a master and apprentice."

~ Yoda

WHEN I SEE the *Star Wars* movies, there's always a point where my eyes tear up as I behold the beautiful depictions of the master (Obi-Wan in *Star Wars* and Yoda in *The Empire Strikes Back*) imparting guidance and insight to the apprentice. It's a theme that touches me deeply, since I experienced it myself in real life.

Many students of music today are trying to go it alone and be self-taught, mainly from YouTube. Before the internet was so widespread, there were numerous home study courses in book and DVD formats. But for some reason, because of YouTube, many more people than in the past, forego traditional lessons.

Trying to teach oneself is problematic. Of course, all learning, in the end, is self-learning, but having a real-life teacher or coach is essential. You can't give yourself in-the-moment feedback!

The true teacher offers more than information

In self-study courses, the information you will find is often very good, but even if it is 100% right, it's just a dead pile of information. It's the raw info only. Learning to play music is much more than knowing a pile of information.

The teacher imparts a knowingness which can even be transferred silently. As a student, you can *feel* you are moving along on the right path by being in the presence of someone who knows. The teacher can also be a source of support for when a student hits an obstacle and wants to give up, stay in the comfort zone, or quit.

The teacher is the living, breathing example of someone who passed through the same difficulties, got around the same obstacles, and passed through the same fires that the student faces. It is precisely this support that can help the student hang in there, or course-correct so that she may become a master one day herself.

All of the arts and many trades have a tradition of the master-apprentice relationship. Whether it's music, writing, woodworking, painting, dance, martial arts, or culinary skills, all crafts are learned best under the eyes of a teacher. A good teacher gives the raw information, but also guides the student through the training and offers immediate feedback and correction.

Just recently one of my online students uploaded a beautiful solo-guitar version of the Beatles' "Yesterday." I was able to offer some feedback where in two spots he had a fingering habit that made him unknowingly push the beat ahead, and leave a melody note out. This was a blind spot for him, even though the rest of the piece was perfectly played. I was able to give supportive feedback and correction and open his eyes and ears to a new level of listening.

This is just one small example. Now consider if he were going it alone. He could have gone on for the rest of his life playing "Yesterday" wrong, unaware of his blind spot. Now he's aware of the mistake he made, and he now knows how to listen and correct himself so that mistake doesn't occur again, in this piece and in future pieces as well.

The greatest musicians in the world all had teachers and took lessons. It's not sexy or cool to think that the greats took lessons and did hard work in spite of being extremely gifted. The reality would certainly make for a boring movie plot.

For example, Mozart was a young master, yet he enjoyed a mentorship with the older Hadyn. Bach apparently studied with an organist named Georg Böhm. Beethoven studied with Christian Gottlob Neefe, who taught him composition.

The three stages of artistic development

There are three stages of artistic development:

- Imitation
- Realization
- Maturity

It's helpful to understand these three levels of learning and development so that you can place yourself properly and not stay stuck in your evolution.

Stage one: imitation

When a little kid learns to speak, they are imitating what they hear, most likely from their parents. It's practice for them; they are going through the motions that someone else has laid out.

Imitation is often the indication of a high degree of talent. It does not necessarily indicate a true level of understanding, though.

How many child actors have we seen who appear funny because they do adult-like things? The humor lies in the paradox of a little kid having what appears to be the experience and the insight of an adult. When children imitate adults, it's surface level, and the child has no real grasp of what it is they are suggesting.

This can be confusing for them, especially when they then get showered with praise for imitating.

There are many incredible child prodigies everywhere; one can just fire up some YouTube videos and watch them. It's beautiful to see these little kids start to blossom, but imitation is not a place one wants to stay in forever.

For some reason in our current era, imitation is praised and sought after by many aspiring musicians. So many developing musicians have the idea that learning note-for-note versions of songs is the goal. There are even some professional-level musicians who are highly developed imitators yet never pass the imitative stage. It's as if they can pronounce a foreign language perfectly with no idea what the words mean.

The key to graduating up from the imitative phase is to start learning how to use the individual tools and concepts behind the craft.

One must strive to emulate and be like the master rather than copy the master.

My mentor was the illustrious Mike Longo. He told me that when he entered the jazz scene in New York City around 1962, imitation was very much frowned upon by the jazz community. For example, everyone knew the signature sound of people like John Coltrane, Bill Evans, and Charlie Parker. If anyone played in a way that copied those distinct musical voices, the community would feel that person was simply an imitator. It was an indication that they could not really get into the ring and deal with a real-life musical situation, because they were in a bubble of attempting to sound like their favorite record.

Today with the advent of all the music schools and online videos, imitation is highly encouraged, which is a pity.

A true master-teacher will encourage the student to find their own inner voice and get it to come through, rather than imitate. This is called realization.

Stage two: realization

The level of realization happens when the student starts to learn and understand the underlying concepts and forces involved in their art, rather than only imitate.

In music, the dawning of realization begins when one learns about the physics of music: rhythm, harmony, melody, technique, and so on. Only when these seeds are planted will the student be able to grow his own musical garden. Otherwise, that same musician could end up being an imitative playback device for the rest of their life.

A deep level of realization comes simply when one listens to their own sound on the instrument while following the musical "laws of physics."

When one is obeying musical physics, one cannot imitate. Allow me to explain.

Rhythm obeys the laws of physics much like riding a bicycle does. If you're riding a bike, are you imitating someone? Of course not! You can't. It's impossible. Sure, you can imitate another bike rider's facial expressions, sounds, or fashion choices, but the pure, physical act of staying balanced on a bike is something one must realize internally though physics. The "aha" moment one has, when they first figure out how to balance on a bike and not tip over, cannot be learned through imitation.

Playing music properly is like that.

When you're playing properly, imitation is impossible. What's left over when you don't imitate? Your unique voice! The real you shines forth even if you are not aware of it. It's effortless. You need not *try* to be original or different. You are already one of a kind.

Stage three: maturity

Musical maturity happens after one has been brewing in the realized stage for some time. At that point, thousands of micro-decisions regarding touch, time, tone, and taste have been thought about and digested.

Once they are digested, they simply become one's way of being, and you need not think about every move.

When you hear a mature musician such as B.B. King, for example, you know it's him when he plays one note. The attack, the holding of the tone, the speed of the vibrato, the bend, and the decay were once all decisions that he had to make.

There may be ten-thousand imitators, but there is only one B.B. King. (And there's only one *you*, too!)

A mature musician is aware of the possibilities and knows the lay of the land, but they know first and foremost that their sound, instinct, and groove will always lead to the right place.

Warning: A musician may say in an interview things like "I just feel it" or "I have no idea what I am doing." When a student reads such things, it can be misleading. If a musician is only a performer, they might not be aware (or care about) how to articulate ideas clearly for beginners and then end up saying things like "just feel it."

Yes, from the top of the mountain this makes perfect sense. Once one is in a mature phase and in command of their own sound and way to play, little conscious thought is involved. It feels as if the music plays itself at that stage.

It can also be very misleading advice to the beginner student who has not yet even approached the realized phase. A student who is in need of concrete concepts has to do more than rely on feelings.

Feelings versus knowledge

Mike Longo used to tell me, "Feelings are what you get out of the music, not what you put into it." If you are like me (and I bet you are) when you listen to music, you want to ultimately feel something. Or you might say "player A is great technically, but player B has a better *feel.*"

Whether it's jazz, country, funk, classical, hip-hop, or even heavy metal, the feel of the music is all-important.

Some music is intellectually stimulating. Some is interesting. Sometimes the speed itself can make things very interesting, but in the end it has to feel good.

What is a feeling?

A feeling is a byproduct, a reaction to a thought or a group of thoughts. Often it is unconscious, nonverbal, and saved in the body rather than the mind (such as when you have a "gut" feeling about something). A feeling can also serve you as a shortcut so you don't have to think all the same thoughts again, step by step.

Think of the sensation of a feeling the same way you'd think of tasting a flavor in your mouth.

1. The chef at a fine restaurant prepares the dish you are about to eat.

2. The food arrives; you put a bite of it into your mouth.

3. The information is received by your taste buds.

4. You experience the phenomena of taste and flavor as a byproduct and result.

Flavor was not an ingredient that the chef put in. It was an experience you had as a reaction or result.

Professionals don't rely on feelings

If the chef himself has a job at a five-star restaurant, he must deliver his signature dishes to customers on demand. Three-hundred-sixty-five days a year, he might experience a variety of feelings ranging from happy to sad, alert to tired, physically stiff to loose, and so on. Yet the day-after-day consistency of his fine cuisine is required, no matter how he feels.

Were this chef to rely only on feelings or spontaneous random whims for the food to taste right, he'd likely fail and be out of a job. But with the sword (or spatula) of knowledge, he can perform consistently night after night and live up to the restaurant clientele's expectations.

Have you ever seen a beautiful, gothic cathedral, such as Notre Dame in Paris, Saint Stephan's Cathedral in Vienna, or the Cathedral of Saint John the Divine in New York City? These structures are breathtakingly beautiful, but the feeling one gets from beholding them is not what was required to engineer the building of them!

Professionals in all walks of life do not rely on feelings. That means musicians as well. Feelings are nice, but professionals rely on knowledge, processes, and practice.

For example, if I fly for six hours and I'm hungry and jet-lagged with a stiff neck, I can't hope or guarantee that I will be in a certain emotional state for a performance. My feelings are too unreliable.

That means I have to be able to deliver a good show regardless of how I feel.

When I use the proper playing techniques, I may start to feel something or I may not. But as is often the case, the audience feels something even when I don't due to the preparation, study, and practice I have done ahead of time.

The cycle and mechanics of playing with feeling

In no way am I advocating cutting off from emotions, or suggesting that you play music from your intellect and ignore the heart.

I have described how an audience member might feel an emotion or feeling as a byproduct of music we create. How should *we* feel when we play? How does "playing with feeling" actually work?

Here is the process of playing with feeling:

- You play a note (or notes)
- You listen deeply to the sound
- Your musical instinct informs you where the music needs to go next
- Before any intellectual thought enters… go back to top of list!

This cycle happens extremely fast— like in thousandths of a second.

Play-listen-react, play-listen-react, play-listen-react, etc.

We call that playing with feeling.

In fact, it happens at such a fast rate of vibration that it almost just feels like a state of openness to emotions, ideas, and music all at once. On the micro-level, however, there is this fast alternation between playing, listening, and reacting.

It's a lot like driving a car. When you drive down the highway in a straight path, it's actually not straight. There are thousands of times that you unconsciously steer the wheel to the right or left as course-correcting moves in order to stay on your "straight" path. Driving straight feels like a singular flow, but it's made up of a high alternating vibration of left and right turns, maybe too small to even detect.

Can you start with feelings?

I'd like you to imagine that you are a guitar teacher. A six-year-old kid walks into your teaching studio for her first guitar lesson.

And then you say, "You have to just feel it. Let your emotions lead you."

Huh? Are you kidding? You'd either lose your clients or, if you were at a music school, you'd be out of a job for sure. And the parents might report you to the police. :-)

Let's rewind that scenario.

A six-year-old kid walks into your teaching studio for her first guitar lesson.

After making her feel safe and secure you say, "Why don't you take out the guitar?" She then proceeds to hold it upside down.

You gently and kindly say, "Here let me show you how to hold it" and set it in her hands properly.

Can you see how futile it would be to tell a six-year-old to use emotions to play? The six-year-old needs *knowledge* first.

Watch out for the feeling trap

There's a trap that the self-taught musician can fall into. It looks something like this:

- Student becomes aware of a new skill to develop (example: learn music theory).

- Student finds online materials to be an overwhelming pile of information.

- Student is alone, with no teacher to demonstrate the tie-in to real music.

- Student gets pushed out of comfort zone and feels uncomfortable.

- Student wants to feel good again, falls back into playing what he knows, and drops the unpleasant study.

- Student justifies his actions by saying, "I don't like that intellectual stuff. I just play by feelings."

Even worse is when that student reads or hears an interview of a musical icon who endorses "just playing with feelings" and proudly talks about how they have no education and can't read music.

This only makes the student feel justified in not learning.

The logic is like this: "I play good because I'm dumb, so I don't want to get smarter because my dumbness helps me play good."

Don't be this person, please!

Knowledge hangs out in the background and guides you when you are in a *play-listen-react* cycle. This is similar to how you know vocabulary words and have them on reserve in your mind, but when you are in a conversational flow you are doing a *listen-react-speak* cycle, and the correct vocabulary words appear in your mind so that you may express your ideas—as if by magic.

The takeaway

Music is a craft that is best studied with a teacher. A teacher can help you see and hear things that you can't perceive when you're making the music yourself; there may be blind spots.

Feelings and emotion are a murky subject. The key thing to remember is that feelings are a byproduct, not an ingredient.

We all love music that feels good, but being the creator is different than being the consumer. As musical creators it is our duty to gain the necessary knowledge, and then use it in a way that is aesthetically and emotionally pleasing (and hopefully makes us feel good too!)

Playing with feeling is actually a lightning-fast cycle of *play-listen-react*. It repeats so fast that it's akin to a frequency, and one feels as if the music is actually coming as a result of emotions and feelings.

Knowledge of music is essential and waits patiently in the background. It is there so that you can enrich and expand the *play-listen-react* cycle even more.

Often when we experience music, we take the whole of it in and let our souls be touched without thinking too much about it. That's good, and that's how it should be!

Like any area of study, music is actually made up of separate areas of study. They are like building blocks, and each one is an area of study unto itself.

Let's take a closer look at them, one by one.

Chapter Five

The Ten Areas of Musical Study

"You ask what is the use of classification, arrangement, systematization? I answer you: order and simplification are the first steps toward the mastery of a subject. The actual enemy is the unknown. "

~ Thomas Mann

"You brought a notebook?" Mike asked.

"Yes," I answered.

"Good. Open it up, and write the following at the top of the page: The Ten Areas of Musical Study."

That was how my first lesson with Mike began. What he then laid out for me is the most intelligent and comprehensive breakdown of music I have ever seen. It contained everything in ten items, with left nothing out.

His masterful overview of music was in stark contrast to how I'd been taught in college for the two preceding years.

What to play and how to play

I will now lead you through the list of the ten areas of musical study, and I'd like you to write this out (not just read it) so you can experience what I did at that lesson.

At the very top of the page write the header: "Ten Areas of Musical Study."

Under that, make two columns. On the left, we'll have "What to Play" and on the right side, "How to Play."

Under "What to Play," write the following:

- Harmony
- Melody
- Rhythm
- Counterpoint
- Form

Under "How to Play," write:

- Touch
- Time
- Tone
- Technique
- Taste

I like the overview when it is shown as a table rather than a list:

The Ten Areas of Musical Study

What to Play	How to Play
Harmony	Touch
Melody	Time
Rhythm	Tone
Counterpoint	Technique
Form	Taste

What's so great about this list?

What I love about this list is that one can shine a laser beam of focus on one subject and not fear that the other subjects will be forgotten.

My school experience was such that we'd study harmony but have a million murky questions about the other nine areas.

With this list, you'll know that if you are studying harmony, the other nine items will wait patiently for you and will be fully addressed when the time is right.

Technically speaking, *this list chilled me out.*

Column one: what to play (a closer look)

Here's the part of the list that is concrete and quantifiable. Most of the basic information here is available in many books and is taught in schools. However, there are some common misunderstandings that I will do my best to dispel.

What to play #1: harmony

What is harmony?

Harmony is commonly thought of as "chords." Guitarists can often get a quick jumpstart on playing by learning a few chord "shapes" with their left hand. With a few common chord shapes, one can literally write and play thousands of songs. That is how I started.

Unfortunately, those left-hand grips or shapes also lay the groundwork for deep misunderstandings about harmony. You won't see it at first, but this misunderstanding will creep up on you slowly. It's as if you were painting a floor, and everything seemed fine until you were backed into a corner, with no way out other than walking on the fresh paint.

Allow me to explain how learning "guitar chords" may confuse you later on.

When you watch one second of a movie, you are actually seeing twenty-five still images flash in rapid sequence. They are shown fast enough that the eye perceives the characters and scenes on the screens as "moving" on the screen. More importantly, you perceive a storyline and a plot, and this is all conveyed through showing one still image at a time.

Imagine now that we cut one of those images out and look at it. In the old days this would have been one frame of film.

Can we possibly know anything about the characters, the plot, the storyline, from observing this still image? Of course not. The context of this image depends on what came before it, what comes after it, and its placement in the overall flow of the story.

This still frame may even show all the main characters, but without the proper context, we have no idea of its meaning.

That's how most people think of chords and harmony. Standalone chords are just like cut-out images in a movie. "If I just play these notes together, they'll harmonize and sound okay. I'll memorize that shape." The problem is, those shapes have to relate to one another within the flow of music.

A better way to describe harmony is actually "motion."

Rather than see chords as simply a pile-up of notes that sound good together at a single moment in time, let's imagine four voices singing four independent melody lines flowing through time. Think of the voices as you would think of four characters flowing through the storyline of a movie.

Here's the beauty of traditional harmony. If you were to stop the flow and observe or analyze what the four voices were singing at a single moment in time, you'd most likely find that the four notes also harmonize perfectly with each other—and we call that a chord (in traditional music).

Harmony starts with melody

Harmony actually started with the flow of melody as its basis.

Old medieval melodies and Gregorian chants were simple melodies that monks would sing in unison (meaning, they'd all sing the same note.)

Some monks would sing a 5th away by mistake, but it sounded pretty good! The natural overtones of a note can very easily lead one to singing these. In fact, I have heard this exact musical mistake at many birthday parties when the guests sing "Happy Birthday."

So, once the monks got the sound of the 5th intervals in their ear, they'd sing the melodies with two notes: the main melody, and a second parallel melody a 5th away.

It did not take long for the monks with a musical inclination to discover yet another note that sounded good with these 5th structures, the 3rd. So a 3rd was then added in the bottom voice and each note in the chants had three notes: the main melody and two notes under it moving in parallel motion. A triad was born.

This style of melody with triads moving in parallel was called *organum*. The reason I've explained this from the ground up is to illustrate that harmony was born from melodic flow.

A very common mistake is that musicians think harmony is a pile of notes built from a bass note up. It is better thought of as a melody note, and then the harmony is built down from there.

By the time Bach was using harmony, it was far more advanced than organum. Rather than all voices moving parallel to one another, voices could move in a variety of different directions and use different rhythms to create a more satisfying and spacious, independent "3D" effect.

Bach was insistent on his students mastering the art of what is called *voice leading*. In this technique, if a harmony is written with four notes, each of those notes is treated like a human voice. As the harmonic progression moves forward through time and the harmonies change, each "voice" must always remain a singable melody.

This is a more horizontal, flowing approach to harmony than most of us are taught. Commonly, we are told to think of chords as a pile of notes stacked up vertically over a bass note. However, if you listen to a beautiful choir or orchestra closely, you'll hear how every note in a harmony leads smoothly into the next harmonious note. That's voice leading.

One of Bach's basic rules for his students was that if they started a harmonization with four voices, they couldn't simply plop a five-note chord in just because the combination of notes "sounded good." That would be like four singers suddenly becoming five singers, which, of course, is impossible.

Bach would even poke fun at keyboardists who disregarded voice leading and just played big, loud, note-filled chords. He called them "knights of the piano."

When Bach taught voice leading to students (on the keyboard and on paper as well), he would take a well-known chorale melody (a short church hymn), and he would write the melody and add a bassline.

It was then the students' homework assignment to fill in the middle-two voices (alto voice is under the soprano, and tenor is between the bass and alto). In the end, it would be a four-voiced harmonic progression.

I myself studied harmony like this under Mike's watchful eye, doing the same type of exercises. I can remember once doing an exercise I thought was 100% correct—everything sounded perfect to my ear. He gazed at it for about seven minutes in silence, hearing it in his head.

Then he said, "Do you have an eraser?" He proceeded to simply swap out two of the notes in the alto and tenor that I had written in. Meaning, in one chord he simply juxtaposed the position of two notes.

The result? The flow of the alto and tenor melodies in the horizontal sense was improved 100%. After his adjustment, you could sing each voice more easily; they both flowed like little songs. I had not perceived the weakness previously, because I was thinking about the vertical chords more than the horizontal flow.

I got that tickle in my solar plexus and laughed. The music was now even more "right," and my teacher had simply uncovered the solution.

So harmony is one of the basics. I've taught some basic voice-leading moves to many students, and they've come back to me months later saying things like, "I'm starting to hear all this new stuff," "I can come up with guitar parts for my band that fit perfectly," and best yet, "I'm writing new tunes based on what you showed me."

It really pays to go deep into this study, rather than go wider and simply play more music at the same level of understanding one is currently at.

Putting in my time in with a cup of coffee, a music notebook, and a pencil, I've solved many harmony and counterpoint problems as if they were chess moves I had to think through. That does not result in "licks," but what stays is a knowingness and a vigilance not to write sounds that are unpleasing.

And there's another benefit to written musical work: you learn to get the sound in your ear and write it down, much as you would speak inwardly while writing text, much like what I'm doing now in front of my computer screen.

It's not that you write music with an intellectual idea and then find out what it sounds like later. Mike would always remind me: "You go from the sound to the paper, not the other way around."

What to play #2: melody

A melody is a series of single notes that are like a connect-the-dots drawing. The result is the sonic effect of what is called a *melodic line*.

A melody should be singable. Even fast, complex melodies by the masters of jazz are singable and quite lyrical. It's just tricky for a non-jazz ear to hear them clearly, which is understandable.

In terms of composing a melody, the *sense of a song* in one's inner ear is almost impossible to explain. A melody is born of a "germ" and has a life of its own and can't be arrived at intellectually. It's a gift from above, and you have to just channel it.

I don't always receive melodies, but when I do, it's best if I drop everything that I'm doing and write the song down right then and there. Or sing it into a voice memo app on my phone so I don't forget it.

For example, we've all played a simple, single note repeated several times, right? But if a composer is open to receiving a melody, it will sound to them like a germ of a song and can then be fleshed out.

A repeated melody note has given birth to songs like the Beatles "Back in the USSR," Paul McCartney and Wings' "Silly Love Songs," Cole Porter's "Every Time We Say Goodbye," and Jobim's famous "One-Note Samba."

And a repeated note is, of course, just one, limited possibility.

So, first and foremost, a melody should "sound like a song" and not just be a series of any notes.

Great melodies stand the test of time

A great melody will stand the test of time. And a great melody could be played by a flute on a street corner and be completely recognizable.

Consider the following melodies. I bet they will be here in two-hundred years (assuming our planet still is):

- "Yesterday," by the Beatles
- "You Are the Sunshine of My Life," by Stevie Wonder
- "Every Breath You Take," by Sting
- "Eine Kleine Nachtmusik," by Mozart
- "Jesu, Joy of Man's Desiring," by Bach
- Beethoven's Fifth Symphony (main theme)

Melody is the identifying factor in music

I see so many funk bands, dance bands, African groups, and fingerstyle percussive guitarists who do great rhythmic things that are fun to watch and groove to, but without melody, nothing sticks other than the memory that the performance was "a nice experience," "cool," or "interesting."

Some artists even leave melody out as if it's something uncool, unhip, and that only old-fashioned musicians use.

The fact is, coming up with a good melody is not so easy. One must be vigilant for when the song arrives and act on it when it does.

It's unfortunate when singer/songwriters write great lyrics but just kind of sing whatever melody notes are comfortable for them, because they think the text has enough meaning to carry the music. That indicates that there was no melodic germ, and it's as if there were simply some sing-song musical pitches assigned to talking.

Sometimes melodies will arrive by accident. You can be fumbling on an instrument and you hit something, and the notes jump out and say to you, "Hey, I could be a song!" Melodies can show up when you least expect them.

Seek to avoid melodic weaknesses

Even when you have a great start to a melody, there are some weaknesses to be on the lookout for.

Here are a few basic guidelines that will keep you out of melodic trouble:

- Don't encircle one tone too much. Imagine if you have one note and you sing a little higher, come back, a little lower, come back, and keep doing that. It can get very aggravating and start to sound weak. It's very subjective, but be aware that this can be a problem.

- Draw the shape of the melodic line like a line, on paper. A very effective melody will tend to have one high point and one low point, and a nice clear shape. Maybe it will go up, up, up and drop down—or maybe it will climb down and come back up. Just like looking off at a mountain range from a distance, it's very pleasing to see one mountain that's tallest and has a clear shape.

- Repeated notes are, of course, the easiest to sing. Stepwise motion between notes is the easiest type of motion to sing, and very effective in making a smooth line. A scale, for example, is stepwise motion (half or whole steps), which on a guitar is either one or two frets. A good melody has repeated notes, stepwise notes, and a few leaps to spice it up.

- If you sing a big interval leap, try to step back in the opposite direction.

Nerdy music stuff coming… Okay, this may sound abstract, and if you can't follow this, don't worry about it. I bet you know the sound in any case.

Sing the first three notes of "Somewhere Over the Rainbow."

"Some" leaps up an octave on the word "where" and steps back a half-step on the "o" of "over." Can you see it in your mind's eye? Big leap up and a half-step down.

Same idea applies for the other direction as well. If you know the old song, "The Way You Look Tonight," the first three notes do the following: the lyric "some" leaps down a 5th to "day" and steps up to "when."

If a melody does two leaps in a row, it can start to lose the linear quality—the exception being if you are arpeggiating a chord.

An arpeggio-melody example is the first seven notes of "The Star-Spangled Banner" ending on the word "by," and then it starts to do some stepwise motion.

Should you first write the melody or the chords?

There's more than one right answer to that, and more than one right way to do it.

If you're a composer or songwriter, this is an interesting

question. There are certainly bluesy songs where the accompaniment has such a good feel that one can plop a little riff up top, and that will suffice for part of the melody.

I'm willing to bet that a song like Stevie Wonder's "Superstition" was a riff-first/melody-second type of song.

Experienced musicians and composers hear a flow of music, and I think the harmony and melody reveal themselves at the same time. For example, "We Are the Champions," by Queen is a song where I can't imagine melody and harmony written separately, but clearly the inspired part of the song is the chorus where they sing the hook (chorus) with the lyric "We are the champions."

I'm willing to bet that the hook was "received" first as the inspired germ of the song, and the verse was written afterwards. (Sometimes the middle of the song comes to you first, and you must work your way back to the beginning.)

Several chord possibilities

A single melody note can be harmonized with many different harmonies, so a bad, backwards way to do it is to write a chord progression and then search for melody. That usually doesn't end well, so I emphatically say: don't write the chords first. When in doubt, go with melody first, and you can always mess with chords after the fact. (Chords are color; melody is line.)

What to play #3: rhythm

What is rhythm? The word comes from the Greek term *rhythmos*, meaning "symmetry" or "any recurring, regular motion." It has been described as a movement marked by the succession of strong and weak elements.

Rhythm can be seen in nature's cyclical events. Units of time (such as milliseconds, seconds, minutes, days, weeks, months, seasons, years, and even centuries) are all rhythms. Some of these may be too fast or too slow for us to perceive as rhythms, but they are rhythms all the same.

Nature also offers many rhythmic sounds, such as birds cawing and flapping wings, horses galloping, and animals vocalizing. The recognition and understanding of these sounds probably helped our ancestors hunt, survive, and avoid danger in the jungle.

The most basic rhythm a human can play would be a heartbeat-like thump, over and over, like counting "1, 1, 1, 1," and so on. We can assume that's how musical rhythm probably started, since it can't get much simpler than that. *That's the pulse.*

As music evolved, musicians started to realize they could play these rhythms in groups of two, three, four, and even other groupings as well. These groupings evolved into beats, where "1" tended to be the strongest beat, with other beats weaker in varying degrees.

You can experiment with this yourself, right now. Just say "1, 2, 3," over and over with an emphasis on "1." You'll notice that beat "1" feels stronger than beats "2" and "3."

When music has a pulse at the basis, vocalists and instrumentalists will add decorative melodies and rhythms on top of it to provide interest. One of music's eternal challenges is to play melodies and rhythms against the basic pulse, yet keep the pulse as a reliable, unwavering flow that can still be felt throughout the music.

A simple example of rhythms against a pulse can be heard in the Christmas song "Jingle Bells." Using the chart below, try patting your foot steadily using the count in the left column, and sing the corresponding words in the column on the right. Your foot and the first syllable of the word should "hit" at exactly the same time.

Try to notice how some of the two-syllable words create rhythms that actually occur between your foot thumps. For example, the second syllable of "jingle" happens between foot thumps, when your foot is doing an "up" motion.

Pulse	Decorative
1	Jingle
2	Bells
3	Jingle
4	Bells
1	Jingle
2	all the
3	Way
4	*(vocal silence, thump only)*

And here's another interesting "rhythmic fact": a musical note is also a rhythm! Although it seems to be a steady sound, and thus devoid of rhythm, it actually is a sound vibrating at a very rapid pace. A musical note only *appears to be* **steady.**

This is similar to fluorescent lights, which appear to produce a steady light when, in fact, they flicker on and off at pace so rapid as to be undetectable.

When you sing a note, that's actually just a very rapid rhythm. When a sound vibrates four-hundred-forty times a second, we hear that as the note "A." We refer to such a designated vibration as *pitch*.

Have you ever thought about how the word frequency is used to describe a sound? In a recording studio, an engineer adjusts the high, middle, and low frequencies. When we say "frequency," we're actually describing how frequently a vibration is happening. So frequency is actually also a rhythm.

At this point you may be asking, how do feeling and groove fit into this purely mathematical concept of rhythm?

Here goes…

When groups of people experience rhythm collectively, they tend to lose the feeling of being separate individuals and unite into a collective, shared identity. This shared-identity concept from rhythm helped ancient armies to fight: the rhythmic war cries, rhythmic drumming, and rhythmic marching would put the warriors into a "battle trance."

And this is the tipping point at which the mathematics of rhythm evoke a feeling. We start to feel an emotional reaction to rhythm. This is the birth of what we call "groove." When we experience a rhythmic pulse, combined with a collective group energy, our deepest feelings of human connection arise.

When many musicians and music teachers attempt to teach how a student can reverse-engineer this process and "put the groove into the music," their suggestions and teachings are problematic, as they tend to be based on superstition and pseudo-science.

Groove is a very tricky subject, because feelings are not quantifiable, and no two people feel music or rhythm the exactly same way. In fact, some discussions I've had about developing one's rhythm have gotten as heated as discussions about religion or politics. That's because it turns into a belief system, and people tend to identify themselves with their beliefs.

We will discuss how to develop one's groove in the "how to play" section later on in this chapter.

What to play #4: counterpoint

Counterpoint is the art of placing one melody line against another.

Composers study it like a science, but even someone singing a simple melody and strumming a guitar is using counterpoint. Once there are two musical forces happening at the same time, there's counterpoint. It's worth it to investigate how they will fit together in a musically pleasing way.

Counterpoint is a craft that requires awareness, practice, and training. It's as essential to good music as perspective is to art.

Why is it called counterpoint?

Gregorian chant was a form of single-line, unaccompanied vocal music that was the basis of church music during the medieval period (the fifth to the fifteenth centuries). On paper, the notes in the melodic line were written as "points."

As I described earlier, singers and musicians started to discover note combinations that sounded good together. Some two-note combinations sounded harmonious and pleasing to the ear.

The distance between two notes is called an *interval*. For example, a C jumping up to the next highest C is the "leap" of an octave (8ve). That's called a *melodic* interval, since it is a step or leap in a melody.

If we played (or two singers sang) both C's at the same time, that sound would be called a *harmonic* interval. Each harmonic interval has a character of sound. Pleasing intervals are called consonant, and less-pleasing ones are called dissonant.

Composers would start with a single-line melody, each melody note being a point.

They'd then compose a second set of points against the first set, and these were called "counterpoints." For every one melody note, they'd write a single counterpoint. (This is known as 1:1 "species" counterpoint.)

The goal is to write a counterpoint melody line that not only harmonizes with the first line perfectly, but is a melody line on its own. The trick is that you are only allowed to use certain notes, so making a nice melody line is quite a challenge.

Mike used to say, "Each melody has a perfect counterpoint out there waiting to be revealed. Our job is to reveal *the* counterpoint."

When you uncover the perfect counterpoint to a melody, it's like solving a Sudoku puzzle or Rubik's cube. Everything falls into place, and the solution smacks of perfection.

Techniques to make the lines sound contrasting and independent developed further. Instead of simple 1:1 counterpoint (one note written against one note), composers began to add more notes against a single note.

They'd also write different rhythms to each melody line to make it sound even more "conversational."

J.S. Bach: a master you should know

The almighty J.S. Bach is considered to be one of the absolute masters of composition and counterpoint.

When you look closely at the moves of Bach, they are absolute genius. Even the littlest moves he does are amazing. Anything you can glean from his music will surely strengthen your concept, no matter what style you play.

All the other great composers mastered counterpoint as well, but the independent lines are especially pronounced in Bach's music.

Four kinds of motion between voices

When you have two melodic lines playing at the same time, there are four kinds of motion which can be used between them.

If you have never considered these, it will raise your musical concept once you become aware of them.

1. *Contrary motion:* The melody lines move in opposite directions. One melody moves upward and the other moves downward. This is the best type of motion to express independence between the voices.

    In the line drawing below, you can envision the top melody line ascending and the bottom line descending.

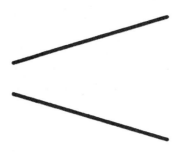

The opposite would also be contrary motion. The top line descends while the bottom line ascends:

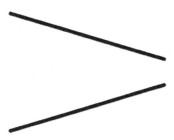

2. *Oblique motion:* This is the next-best method of making melody lines sound independent. One melody line stays put while the other moves in ascending or descending motion. In this illustration, the top line stays and the bottom descends.

3. *Parallel motion:* Both melody lines move exactly parallel to each other. This technique must be used with caution. It's great to have the voices do this briefly, but if

it lasts too long the lines lose their sound of independence.

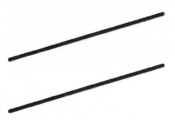

4. *Similar motion:* Both lines move in the same direction but at a different rate. For example, one line moves up step by step like a scale, while the other makes big leaps.

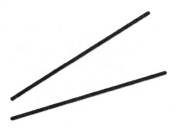

No matter how casual your music making is, you can be on the lookout for these four types of motion. Good pop, jazz, and rock music pay attention to the direction of lines.

In fact, the famous guitar intro to "Stairway to Heaven" uses contrary motion!

To get started with this idea in your music, look at the outer (lowest and highest) voices in whatever music you are playing.

For example, if you are in a band, consider the vocal line and the bass line. If you play fingerstyle guitar, consider your bass line and your melody line.

Try to get those outer voices moving in opposite directions whenever possible. Your music will achieve a more 3D-effect from this simple hack!

Rhythmic counterpoint

Often when musicians start to learn to jam with each other, they'll think they are communicating when they play the exact same thing together. Actually, that's just doubling the same musical idea rather than playing a complementing and contrasting idea.

This can be problematic.

Just imagine: if two people talked at the same time, that could never turn into a conversation. Even worse, if two or more people said the exact same thing at the exact same time, individual voices would be barely discernible, and no one would be listening.

A more effective way to play music is by using *rhythmic counterpoint.*

Rhythmic counterpoint happens when contrasting rhythms are played against each other, so there's plenty of room for everyone to be heard.

- One voice can lay out entirely while the other plays.

- One voice can hold a long note while the other voice plays shorter, faster notes.

- Both voices can be equally active, contrasting with each other perfectly, the way a salsa dancing couple does different moves, but working as a team.

When Dizzy Gillespie composed songs like "A Night in Tunisia," he used rhythmic counterpoint. Prior to Dizzy, jazz had more of a chugga-chugga, old-timey sound.

In "A Night in Tunisia," the bass has its own rhythmic melody, and the piano comping fits perfectly against the bassline. The trumpet melody sings, sailing over the top, in full agreement with the accompaniment. All the parts mesh like gears.

This quantum leap in musical concept that Dizzy revealed led to what we now find today in great jazz, pop, and rock music.

Arranging for solo guitar

When I arrange for solo guitar, I think basically the same way I'd think if I were arranging for a band.

- I'll keep an eye on the outer voices to make sure the directions of lines are contrasting.

- I'll keep an eye on the rhythmic counterpoint.

- I'll put something in the middle to fill the space between the top and bottom.

- I'll think three parts: top, middle, and bottom.

What to play #5: form

Form is the invisible sense of organization in music that brings balance, cohesion, and satisfaction to music. Think of form as "structure."

For example, the designers of a gothic Cathedral may have had a specific design idea for a Roman-style column, but it's all the more satisfying when there are at least two matching columns both on the left and right side.

Likewise, if we saw a human being with one eye missing, we'd likely feel a disturbance, as we'd expect to see a second eye. That's an example of how we naturally seek and appreciate good "form."

And… we perceive beauty when there is slight imperfection in the symmetry.

For example, a left eye that is an exact mirror image of a right eye would seem creepy and digital. The natural variation is appealing and adds to the beauty. When we see swans swim across the surface of a lake, we appreciate the uniformity of how they look, but the ever-so-slight variations make watching them all the more captivating.

Making music beautiful with form

When one has a melodic idea, dropping it into a tried-and-true musical structure will help transmute that single idea into a song. That way, people will be able to appreciate, remember, and digest the music.

For example, when I have an idea for a melody, I know I

can make an intelligible and pleasing song out of it if I present the ideas in what musicians call "AABA form."

An AABA song form follows a specific format (with each section usually eight bars long, often resulting in a thirty-two-bar tune):

- A section presents melodic theme
- A section repeats melodic theme
- B section presents new (but related) melodic material
- A section recaps melodic theme

This standard form offers an initial statement or theme, repetition of the theme, a departure from the theme, and then a return to the theme. Without the departure represented by the B section, the tune would sound monotonous to the listener.

A classic example of AABA form is the theme from "The Flintstones." Many songs from the Great American Songbook use this form. Even songs like "Yesterday" and "Every Breath You Take" use aspects of AABA form.

Form sets the ground rules. It helps the listener anticipate what is about to come, and it plays with the listener's expectations and can offer surprise. It offers a mix of the safe, at-home, predictable feeling with exploration into unknown territory.

The germ, the earworm, the hook

In most music, there is a single theme, a melody, or a "hook," that is the central idea. This is especially true in any kind of popular music. Some call this an "earworm"—that little thing that you remember after hearing the song once.

One can also think of this as the "germ" of a musical

composition. (If you ever write a song and people say "I can't stop singing your song!" you may have a hit on your hands!)

An example of an unforgettable hook is "Yellow Submarine," by the Beatles. Another would be "We Are the Champions," by Queen. When you hear them once, they are stuck in your mind forever.

Antecedent and consequent phrases

Even the greatest song ideas will not communicate properly unless they are put in a form that listeners can easily understand.

The way the musical ideas are introduced is very important because they set the foundation on which the music is built. Just like a house, if the foundation is weak, problems will show up later.

For hundreds of years, composers of Western civilization have set a piece of music into motion with "opening" and "corroborating" phrases, also called "antecedent" and "consequent" phrases.

Basically there's a first phrase, and the second phrase follows up and somehow says, "Yes, that first phrase is true." The two melodies often have the same rhythm. Sometimes the notes are the same, sometimes not.

This is the small micro-equation upon which a bigger structure is successfully built.

Allow me to illustrate. Let's look at a limerick-style poem by Edward Lear as an example. Pay particular attention to the first two lines:

There was an old man with a beard *(opening / antecedent phrase)*

Who said, "It is just as I feared! *(corroborating / conse-quent phrase)*

Two owls and a hen, *(development)*

Four larks and a wren,

Have all built their nests in my beard!"

The important thing to note is the feeling of the opening phrase and corroboration by the second phrase. Imagine if it were just the following—it would feel totally off:

There was an old man with a beard *(opening phrase)*

Two owls and a hen, *(development)*

Four larks and a wren,

Have all built their nests in my beard!

Can you see the importance of the corroborating second phrase?

Musical examples of antecedent and consequent phrases

Have you ever listened to Beethoven's Fifth Symphony? There's the famous big, fat, four-note opening "da da da daa"—that's the *antecedent* phrase.

The next "da da da daaa" is the *consequent* phrase, which corroborates the first one. Then the piece develops in complexity after that.

In college, a professor sang us the first (antecedent) phrases of many Mozart pieces we'd never heard and we had to invent and sing back a corroborating (consequent) phrase.

It is often blindingly obvious as to what the consequent

phrase should be. In some cases, we could sing what Mozart wrote even though we hadn't heard the piece before.

This just shows that in many cases one need not *try* to be creative. One can just allow the music to write itself. Like a chess game opening, when white moves his pawn first, it's almost always "answered" by black moving a pawn.

The musical phrases can be short or long. All that matters is that "yes" feeling one gets when the second corroborating phrase is delivered.

Here are some Beatles examples:

Opening phrase *(antecedent)*	Corroborating phrase *(consequent)*
She loves you, yeah, yeah, yeah	She loves you, yeah, yeah, yeah
We all live in a yellow submarine, a yellow submarine, a yellow submarine	We all live in a yellow submarine, a yellow submarine, a yellow submarine

"Yellow submarine" is two repeats of the same phrase. "She loves you" is almost repeated—except the harmony on the second phrase offers a slight variation.

Some opening and corroborating phrases are more like a question and an answer. (You'll have to sing these to yourself to hear the melodies rise and fall.)

Opening Phrase *(Antecedent)*	Corroborating Phrase *(Consequent)*
Happy birthday to you (ends like an unresolved question)	Happy birthday to you (answers the question)
Twinkle, twinkle, little star (part one ascending melody)	How I wonder what you are (part two descending melody)

Some opening and corroborating phrases are more hidden and not in-your-face obvious. Take "Yesterday," for example. The word "yesterday" is corroborated by the lyric "far away." All the words in between are a lead-up to the corroborating element.

Yesterday. All my troubles seemed so	*far away*.

"Superstitious," by Stevie Wonder has longer phrases. The second time you hear the words "very superstitious," at the start of the phrase you experience the corroboration.

Very Superstitious— writing's on the wall.	*very superstitious,* ladders 'bout to fall

Then, just like in Beethoven's Fifth Symphony, the music develops.

Larger song structures

Here are some basic song structures. They are best learned by learning real songs, not simply from reading this book, but here's an overview:

- *Alternating verse and chorus*—examples : "Jingle Bells," "Yellow Submarine," "Hotel California," "Billie Jean"

- *Verses with built-in hook elements* (usually beginnings or endings of phrases)—examples: "Superstition," "My Cherie Amour," "Yesterday," "Every Breath You Take"

- *AABA form* (32 bars) (many *Great American Songbook* tunes and jazz standards follow this common form)— examples: "Blue Moon," "Over the Rainbow," "Georgia," "I Got Rhythm"

When good form is used, there's enough symmetry to make you feel at home, yet just enough variation to keep you interested and on your toes.

That's the magic of form.

How to play: touch, time, tone, technique, and taste

So far we've been talking only about the left side of Mike Longo's diagram, "The Ten Areas of Musical Study." We've been discussing *what* to play: the five "what's" of music making. This information can be learned from just about any music teacher or school and serves as a definition of terms. There's no personal opinion or storytelling involved in the "what."

But now we're going to examine the five elements on the right side of the diagram: the "how" aspect of music making.

This information is harder to define and can't easily be described in a book or taught in a class.

Just so we remember where we're at in this discussion, let's take a peek at that diagram again:

The Ten Areas of Musical Study

What to Play	How to Play
Harmony	Touch
Melody	Time
Rhythm	Tone
Counterpoint	Technique
Form	Taste

Many musicians and music teachers suggest that one can improve "how" one plays through emotions, sexual energy, getting high, or woo-woo spirituality. Some suggest that a certain ethnicity is required for mastery of certain musical forces.

That is superstitious baloney. Playing music properly is based on physics, listening, musical intelligence, and intense concentration—not one's race, gender, emotions, or invocation of spiritual mumbo-jumbo.

Cultural influences do play a role in music, though. For example, someone from India will probably have a better feel for Indian music than I do, since they were exposed to it in early childhood.

Let's take a look now at the five elements involved in "how" to play. I'll do my best to dispel common misunderstandings and shine the light of knowledge for you in the pages ahead.

How to play #1: touch

I think of touch as the sound's "front end of the attack."

Developing one's touch is like developing clearly articulated syllables in speech. Practice of touch must be mindful. It's a combination of paying attention to the sound you make in coordination with the feeling in your hands.

It's easy to mistakenly credit a great guitar sound to the instrument rather than the player. The sound is usually in the hands, not the instrument.

I've heard examples on the drums, for example, where a drum set was played by a student and then played by the teacher. The sounds go from cloudy to clear, and it is readily seen that the clear sound is due to the more experienced player having a better touch.

Each style of music lends itself to a different touch and tone. Dedication to a style and sound of music will lead you to touch your instrument in such a way that you make the right sound for that music. Country music, jazz, classical, rock, and flamenco all have distinctly different touches on the guitar.

On guitar, one has many choices in how to attack the string. With the right hand, one can use a flatpick, fingernails, flesh of the fingers, thumb picks, fingerpicks, and even hammer notes on the fretboard; the left hand can press strings, play pull-offs, hammer-ons, and slides.

It's important for you to try all of them, and allow what feels right to stay, and just allow everything else to fall away. This is not just feel-good advice. There is a deep, spiritual significance in staying with what feels right to you, so that you play from a place of alignment.

Your body has an invisible, inner energy highway. Traditional Chinese medicine calls this energy called "Qi" (pronounced *chee*), and the highway system is called the *meridian system*.

When you perceive something as true, this meridian system (not the muscles) go "strong." When you play music in a way that is your truth, you feel a "yes" feeling in your body, flowing from your innermost being to your fingertips.

How to play #2: time

Playing rhythms is different than playing with rhythm. The mature musician has a heartbeat-like, organic depth to the way she keeps time, even before a note is played.

The concept of a heartbeat-like flow is universal to all great music. The goal of keeping time musically is to give up control of the notes and surrender yourself to the flow.

Yet, one of the most misunderstood aspects of music is rhythm. Many erroneous and superstitious beliefs surround it.

I'll share with you what I can, and will hopefully shed light into some dark corners or at least offer you some new ways of looking at things. This may seriously challenge some of your ideas, so please stay open-minded.

Body rhythm versus head rhythm

Music is usually made up of melodic and harmonic rhythms played on top of a basic pulse. This underlying pulse should be natural and feel like a heartbeat. It's the thing that allows listeners to feel the music in their own bodies, tap their feet, and snap their fingers. Even when the fabric of the music gets complex, one should still be able to feel a basic underlying pulse at the bottom of it all.

When playing an instrument, one should be able to tap one's foot to the basic pulse, and also play the contrasting rhythms of the instrument on top of that. Sometimes I see musicians lose the pulse with their foot. Instead of tapping the pulse, the foot taps the rhythms they are playing on their instrument. That indicates the musician has a problem staying with the pulse they are keeping, and is counting rather than feeling a "heartbeat."

The basic challenge for a musician is this: how can one play melodies and harmonies on an instrument, yet also convey the pulse to the listener?

I'd like to offer the following idea to help clarify the issue. There are two different kinds of rhythm: *body rhythm* and *head rhythm*.

You can count "1, 2, 3, 4" in perfect metronomic time (head rhythm), but that does not necessarily constitute groove (body rhythm).

You might wonder, "How can this be so? Doesn't something groove if the timing is perfect?" Well, not exactly.

Many musicians can play along with a metronome in perfect time, which is a formidable skill, yet the music they produce lacks groove. Many electronic-music dance tracks are manufactured on a computer with software in perfect metronomic time, but don't groove.

Who decides what grooves? Well, you do. It's very subjective. I measure groove by seeing if I start to move my body, tap my feet, and so on. I can only speak for myself.

Stevie Wonder says in the song "Sir Duke": "Just because a record has a groove don't make it in the groove. You can tell what the music's got to say when the people start to move."

So perfect time is a great thing and something we should strive for, but when there's only perfect time in my head and no groove felt in my body, I refer to that as "head rhythm." Ultimately it will never satisfy a listener on a groove level, let alone someone who wants to dance. When songs like this come on in a disco, you can watch the dance floor clear out.

Music by the great classical composers often has a deep, heartbeat-like pulse. Listen to Mozart's "Eine Kleine Nachtmusic," and you can tap your foot the whole way through. It grooves.

I can recall hearing a jazz concert that was a perfect "playback" sound imitation of many great 1960s jazz recordings. I felt nothing in my body listening to these musicians. My foot never started to tap on its own. My musical intellect was extremely satisfied and impressed, yet none of that music made my groove meters light up.

I thought something was wrong with me. I couldn't believe that such perfect playing and excellent musicianship did not feel right. At the time, I wondered if I was crazy. After all, they were playing music perfectly! Now I understand that they were playing head rhythm, not body rhythm.

Playing head rhythm only makes music that is zombie-esque. When we see movies such as "Frankenstein," "Dawn of the Dead," and any Dracula movie in which we see his creepy brides, we see the horror of something *that seems to be animated with life, but is spiritually dead.* These folktales and myths point to real life and illustrate the dangers of eliminating *soul* from our lives.

Body rhythm brings joy. Body rhythm is natural, and effortless.

Many non-musicians are in touch with their body rhythm, sometimes more than the musicians themselves! This can be seen by observing everyday people who go out for a party night of disco dancing. As Mike Longo said, "You can fool the musicians, but you can't fool the people."

Body rhythm can actually be learned and trained. It is based on physics the same way juggling, balancing, or riding a bike is. Some people may have more immediate talent for it than others, but it is learnable.

Art Taylor, the jazz drummer, said, "Never trust a drummer that can't dance."

Rhythm is a behavior

Consider rhythm to be a natural behavior of physics.

It's as if the drummers in Africa discovered and revealed a force in physics, similar to Newton discovering gravity.

After Newton discovered gravity, the concept became available to every human on Earth. The law of gravity does not care about the ethnic background of the person using it.

The physics of rhythm is similar. Rhythm obeys the laws of nature and can be learned, used, and harnessed by any sincere musician regardless of their ethnicity, gender, or religious beliefs.

The West African 'mother rhythm'

One of the greatest musical gifts I have received in this lifetime is learning what Mike calls the "mother rhythm," also known as the "West African drum rudiment." Mike learned this from Dizzy Gillespie during his time with the band.

What he himself gleaned from practicing it was so enlightening and fundamental that he now trains his students with it.

At a certain stage in Dizzy's career, he played quite a bit of conga drums onstage to entertain the crowd. According to Mike, Dizzy did this partially because, as he aged, his teeth were hurting, and this way he could rest his "trumpet chops" and still carry on with the show.

Mike got curious and said "Hey, Diz, show me what you're doing on the conga drum." Dizzy showed him the basic idea, and then Mike, being a scientist, went home and did his research and, of course, practiced what Dizzy had shown him.

An unexpected thing happened. On their next gig, the other musicians were awestruck by Mike's playing, saying things like, "Man, what the heck have you been practicing?" Mike also sensed there were hidden whispers among the other musicians that he, Mike, had "discovered the rhythm secret."

Dizzy looked over at Mike with a twinkle in his eye, knowing full well that showing him the mother rhythm was the planting of a musical seed. It then began to blossom into the huge, conceptual leap on piano that Mike was experiencing.

The mother rhythm is a West African drumming pattern that contains 12/8, 3/4, 6/8, as well 4/4 funk and even 5/4 simultaneously. The twelve-stroke pattern is not just any 12/8, but is a very special set of accents within the 12/8.

When you play this rhythm properly, amazing and profound things start to happen within you. The 12/8, 3/4, 6/8 create what is called a *hemiola*. It sometimes takes a little while for the hemiola to lock in, but when it does, it's as if the drum itself starts talking.

The touch, time, tone, and presence one starts to get playing the drum suddenly take a quantum leap from locking these rhythms in. You literally enter another zone not just in terms of rhythm, but overall presence of your sound.

How the mother rhythm affects your touch, time, and tone

For over ten years, I'd go to my weekly Wednesday 10 am lessons, and Mike would not allow me to play a note on the guitar until I did what he calls "the warm-up." This always started with playing the drum and getting the presence in my sound first.

He would leave his studio to let me play the drum by myself but still listen outside the room. Often he'd come back in after a few minutes and play along with me to get me back on the right track. Through "osmosis," he could transfer to me whatever I was missing.

Once the drum started talking, he allowed me to play guitar, and we'd often play together.

He even did something to fool me one time: he started a lesson by telling me to take out my guitar instead of the drum. "Let's play a blues," he said. He always had a Sony Walkman-style cassette recorder on hand, so he could record lessons.

He started recording, we played the blues, and I thought to myself that it sounded okay.

We finished, and he said, "Pick up the drum." We played, and as usual my initial sound on the drum was muffled and vague, but within minutes the tone had "that ring" and clarity to it.

"Let's play that blues again."

He started recording our second take of the blues. We played, and I perceived nothing different. For me, it just felt like "take two." I didn't make any extra effort to play better or differently. I just did my best, as I had done in the first take.

Then we listened, and I will never forget the mind-blowing experience of it.

The first blues sounded pretty good. But the second one sounded *amazing*.

I say this not in an egotistical sense. I say it as a listener. The second take sounded like a long-lost recording of a wonderful, mature, jazz guitarist no one had ever heard of, and the first one sounded like an eighteen-year-old kid trying to play jazz guitar who still had a few things he needed to learn.

The second recording had a profoundly higher level of touch, time, tone, presence, and depth of groove. This was due to having connected with the deepest part of my being, through the drum.

After experiencing something as profound as this, can you see why I'd feel like the concept of practicing with a metronome is a two-dimensional solution to a three-dimensional problem? There's such a greater spiritual depth to rhythm than playing along to evenly-spaced-out clicks and sounds.

Just the same way that you must tune a guitar before you play, the drum tunes *you* as the instrument. An in-tune instrument has a glow and a presence, and this is precisely what you do to yourself by locking in the African hemiola, the mother rhythm.

How to play #3: tone

Tone is what happens right after touch. It's the singing sustain and swim of the note. Your innermost spirit guides the sound of this note; part of developing your tone involves listening to the sound of your instrument fade into silence.

Developing your tone on your instrument allows your unique voice to emerge. That is your ultimate goal. When one hears Ray Charles, John Coltrane, McCoy Tyner, Jimi Hendrix, Miles Davis, George Benson, Wes Montgomery, Mark Knofler and other masters on any instrument, their sound is identifiable after one note. You know it's them because of their tone.

How to play #4: technique

I have spent my life grappling with and exploring guitar technique. It's fascinating, and it can get unnecessarily complicated.

Here are a few basic guidelines that I hope will make it simpler for you.

Whatever you do technically should be relaxed, cause no pain or discomfort, and enable you to get a sound from your instrument that pleases you. You should be able to play notes in rhythm with ease.

Dizzy Gillespie once said "If it feels stiff, I discard it." That's a pretty good thing to remember!

The perfect solution for someone else may not be a good fit for you, so in this regard I suggest your very own "independent investigation of the truth."

By all means try what teachers show you, and be willing to sit with something new for a while to test it out. New things that take you out of your comfort zone will feel weird. But, in the end, you must remain honest with yourself as to what feels right and what works for you.

However you choose to play should feel like a "yes" to you.

Allow the music to guide your technique rather than have the technique guide your music. It sounds overly simple, but that wisdom is tried and true.

I've made numerous technique changes over the years, and it's always due to letting go of a head-based technical idea and allowing a new concept, groove, or tone to express itself.

Mind your hands

You want to avoid injury to your hands at all costs. Even when you do things correctly, overuse injuries can happen, so any repetitive motions should be practiced for short periods only.

I've never had tendonitis, but I have had times where I felt I pushed my hands to the limit and then had to rest. This has happened when I've become obsessed with "improving" and have not been taking breaks. When I'm in that mode, the mind and ego start to dominate, and I lose contact with my body. That's when injury can occur.

I find that when I play in a true, musical flow and I'm grooving, I have to do so many varied and coordinated movements that I never feel any discomfort. There's no ego-based effort to improve, and I'm not obsessively repeating any physical movements. It's a perfect union of mind and body.

The myth of the crazed, obsessed musician who practices for hours on end is a bad image to hold in mind, and it's just wrong.

There should be no pain or discomfort when you play. You need to take good care of yourself and be mindful at all times.

Overdoing anything is not the way you get better; it's the slow and steady, un-sexy, day-to-day practice that wins the race.

If you've ever seen marathon runners, they don't necessarily look like they are in great shape the way a sprinter does. What marathon runners have discovered is how to do the most efficient movements possible through repetition. It's like "the water has found its own level" over time for their running technique.

Good instrumental technique is similar to that. Be a marathon runner, not a sprinter.

The whip and the crowbar

Imagine if you wanted to hit something with a crowbar. It's a heavy, rigid, steel bar, and after you whack the intended object, you have to hold it stiff to keep it steady in your hands. Overall, that requires force. You couldn't do this for very long without fatigue or injury.

Much easier and smoother is the motion of cracking a whip. With a small, quick motion, an impulse can flow down the whip like a wave and then crack when it gets to the end. Much more efficient, and repeatable.

Your guitar technique—the motion and feeling in your hands and fingers—ought to resemble the whip more than the crowbar, as much less effort is involved. The whip uses power, not force.

You'll have to scan your own playing in real time and ask yourself questions like "Am I using too much strength? Am I tense? Am I forcing my guitar playing? Am I getting fatigued?"

Every great guitar player out there may look as if they are using a different hand position or technique than everybody else, but there is a common thread to the approach of all great players. They stay loose, avoid tension, and make it feel easy for themselves. This often means lightening up one's touch. Great players use power, not force.

Different solutions for different types of music

Allow me to illustrate how there's more than one right way to play the guitar, depending on your inner picture.

If you were to play classical guitar, you'd be taught that your picking-hand fingernails should have a lovely, clear, bell-like attack. That's the first-principle of classical guitar tone.

Classical guitarists strive to make all the fingernails fairly equal in tone quality. If two right-hand fingers sound great and one sounds weak, they'll address the weak tone of that finger to get it up to the level of the other two. They may even grow that fingernail longer.

A totally different first-principle aesthetic exists in jazz. To play jazz, the feeling of swing is of paramount importance. If sounds are produced in a manner that does not fit within the groove, that technique must be discarded. In jazz, one may even use the stronger and weaker sounds from different fingers to shape the music.

Most jazz players don't have a bell-like classical touch, and most classical players don't have the rhythmic "pocket" of a jazz player. This is not an insult or a criticism. It's just like saying soccer players have a similar yet different skillset than basketball players.

(If you've never heard the phrase "in the pocket," it's jazz-player jargon. Being in the pocket means much more than just having good timing. It's a description of a micro-measurement when rhythms are played perfectly and precisely in the groove, much like an arrow perfectly hitting a bullseye on a target.)

So there you have two versions of "right technique." It all depends on your musical values, and especially the groove you intend to play with.

The way I approach guitar technique has evolved through my own first principle, which is to play the guitar with as solid a rhythmic pocket as I can.

This is one of the reasons I teach the "mother rhythm" to students who want to play my groove-based style of solo-guitar playing.

Many students come to me with former training in classical guitar. If they try to learn my techniques using their current concept, it's like putting lipstick on a pig. It doesn't work. They need a new mental picture of rhythm first.

To show students this new picture, I get them to play the mother rhythm on a hand drum. After that, it's just a matter of time for their instrumental technique to shift so that it aligns with their new rhythmic picture.

The moral of the story? Ultimately, your deepest musical intentions guide your technique.

How to play #5: taste

When someone decorates their home "in good taste," it means that out of the thousands of possible choices, they've selected a few that are of good quality and fit together.

To exercise good musical taste, one must have investigated many possibilities beforehand. That's why doing one's musical homework is important, even if it doesn't feel like art when one is studying.

For example, are you aware that there are over ninety-six different possibilities for chord voicings on the chord progression D-7 G7 | Cmaj7 ?

The pianist or guitarist who has taken the time to go through these voicings one at a time, look at the underlying logic, and listen to them intently is then equipped in the flash of an instant, to play the most appropriate "tastiest" chord voicing at the right time. Tasteful choices are made when one is familiar with a wide range of possibilities.

Here's another example of taste I experienced from being in the recording studio.

When I mixed and mastered my solo-guitar CD's with studio legend Gene Paul (son of Les Paul), he did things like:

- Add .5 db treble to one side of the stereo image; toggle on and off to see which sound was more tasteful

- Carefully use multiband compression to make a melody sing out more clearly.

- Use a subtle "small room" reverb, just to make it sound like the mics were a few inches further away from the guitar, to offer a feeling of space

None of these solutions were extreme. These carefully balanced, barely perceivable pinches of flavor helped make the end result all the more satisfying.

That's good taste.

The takeaway

Socrates said, "The beginning of wisdom is the definition of terms." Defining and knowing the elements of music helps one improve the music. The average, casual listener has a binary setting; for them music is either good or bad. They either like it or they don't.

It's our job to take it further, and to get specific so there are no dark corners or stones left unturned.

When we listen to music, we should be able to answer the following questions:

- What are the good qualities in the music?

- What are the weak areas?

- What could stand improvement?

Just the same way that a great athlete may still have a muscle that's in need of training, a talented musician can still have a blind spot. That's why the definition and organization of the elements is so critical. It helps the musician to pinpoint, correct, and strengthen any weaknesses.

Now that we've identified and organized the elements of music, it's time to build a sensible, effective practice routine to address new concepts, strengthen weaknesses, and solidify performance.

Let's take a look at how you can do that.

Chapter Six

How to Practice Guitar Effectively

"The most crucial ingredient by far for success in music is what happens in the practice room."

~ William Westney

IT WAS A sunny springtime Saturday in New York City, 1986. For all the students at our little music school, myself included, it was a very big day.

Little did I know that I'd always remember this day as "The Day I Pooped My Pants."

After months of lessons and diligent preparation, all the students would have the chance to get on stage and perform at the school's end-of-year recital. It was a major event. All the parents, teachers, and other students were expected to attend. Needless to say, it was nerve-wracking.

The recitals would usually start with the littlest kids happily sawing away at "Twinkle, Twinkle, Little Star" on their mini-violins, and then the concert would gradually build up to the older, more advanced students.

At that time, I was fifteen-years-old and deemed to be one of the promising, young, classical guitar students who was destined for music college.

Ten days prior, I had just started learning a piece by Bach (the "Courante" from the Third Cello Suite, in case you are curious) and figured "What the heck. I'll give it a go onstage!"

Mind you, ten days is nowhere near enough prep time for a classical piece. "What could possibly go wrong?" I thought.

I warmed up in a practice room beforehand, and everything sounded pretty good. I was ready.

When the time came and I was called to the stage, I went up, sat down, took a deep breath, and started to play.

But suddenly, it didn't feel like the practice room. People were looking at me, the guitar felt weird, lights were shining in my eyes, and it was hard to think. Uh-oh!

And then the first uncontrollable thought came: "Hey, I played this just a few minutes ago. What's happening to me?" Reptile-brain fight-or-flight mode started kicking in… my heartbeat sped up, and my hands shook involuntarily. I was going off the rails.

Then my mind went completely blank after the first few bars. For the life of me, I could not remember what to play even though I'd played it perfectly in the practice room fifteen minutes before.

An extremely thick and uncomfortable silence descended

upon the room. I made two more futile attempts to start over only to have the same train wreck happen.

I saw parents hiding their eyes with their hands and burying their heads, writhing in the shame I was experiencing.

It was as if I'd pooped my pants, for all to see.

In an attempt to keep the recital flowing along, the music school director came onstage, stood behind me, and placed his hands on my shoulders. He said to the crowd, "Well, well. This can happen to all of us, but now what should we do?"

The cringe-worthiness and self-loathing got deeper and deeper with every second. The skin on my face was burning hot.

He didn't want me to get offstage and leave completely defeated, so he instructed me to play a piece I'd played a thousand times. I got through it, gave a fake smile and bowed, then scurried offstage. The crowd gave me their obligatory applause which cut even deeper. I knew it was fake, and that I really had screwed up.

That day I was the poster child for onstage musical failure. I left with my tail between my legs and licked my wounds for weeks.

It's unfortunate but true: we learn from our most painful experiences.

This was the day I realized that practicing and performing was far more serious business than I had imagined. I had to admit that my preparation was not thorough enough, and my overconfidence did not take into account the different way I would feel onstage.

I was determined to never, ever let that happen again.

Has this ever happened to you?

If it has, it's okay, and you are normal. At many of my live workshops, students will get up to play and have a similar experience.

They feel brand-new, unexpected levels of nervousness. I have heard the sentence "Really, I can play this perfectly at home!" hundreds of times.

If this has ever happened to you, fear not. I understand this better than anyone. I am on your team, and I will show you how to solve this problem.

The four stages of learning

To practice effectively, one must be familiar with the four stages of mastery, also called "the four stages of learning."

Here are the four stages:

- Unconscious incompetence
- Conscious incompetence
- Conscious competence
- Unconscious competence

Let's go through these one by one.

Stage one: unconscious incompetence

This is the point of entry into any skill. You don't know how much you don't know.

Imagine you're in high school. You've been assigned the task of reciting a poem from memory in front of the class two weeks from today.

Your teacher gives you a handout with the text of the poem. You read it over silently a couple of times. You never saw the poem before today. For that matter, you never had to memorize a poem before, either. At first glance, it doesn't seem like a difficult task. You figure reading the poem a few more times ought to be enough for you to remember it.

You are in the stage of unconscious incompetence. You don't know how little you know!

Stage two: conscious incompetence

This is the stage where you become *aware* of how little you know. In the example, it's when you concentrate on memorizing the poem and realize it's a lot harder to do than you thought. You read the poem again and again, and still you can't recite but a line or two from memory. The task seems overwhelming!

You see there's quite a journey ahead. You're conscious of your incompetence. All you can do at this phase is read and reread the material in front of you. It still feels brand-new every time you look at it, and it feels as though nothing is sticking, but you desperately keep plugging away all the same.

Stage three: conscious competence

Next comes the stage where you start to get it. To your surprise, you spontaneously remember whole chunks of the poem when you attempt to recite it. With concentration, you can actually get the entire poem out. When you do have a memory block, all you need is the sound of the next word to get flowing again. It's shaping up. You're almost there!

This is the stage of conscious competence, and it's the

stage where a person is tempted to become overconfident. You think you know the poem better than you actually do. You still depend on concentration to recite the poem correctly. It hasn't become a part of your being yet.

Stage four: unconscious competence

This is the final stage of mastery, where you can be woken up out of a dead sleep, and the performance of a task, or knowledge of a subject, spills out of you effortlessly with no conscious thought.

You don't recite the poem. It's as if the poem recites itself using your voice as the instrument. The words just seem to spill out. And if you feel nervous, thirsty, forgetful, or had a bad morning, none of that even comes into play. The poem isn't only saved in your brain—it's saved in every cell of your body. You observe it happening, being recited *through* you. You watch the poem coming out of your mouth with zero effort, automatically.

You are competent to do the task, even unconsciously, because it's become such a part of you. This is unconscious competence: the fourth and final stage of mastery.

Here's why I pooped my pants

In hindsight, it's fairly easy to see why the train wreck happened at my famous Bach recital.

At that time, I would have said, "But I could play it perfectly at home." But I was at stage three, and I needed to be at stage four in terms of my preparation.

In stage three, you *can* play things perfectly, but only if you can follow the flow with perfect concentration and zero distraction. This is easy to do at home, in your living room, or in a practice room, but it is hardly ever the case when performing live, or in front of a camera or microphone.

If you are in stage three and trying to perform, any bump you experience can easily throw you off-track, and your conscious mind can't recover the flow.

This bump could be anything, such as a small finger-squeak you didn't perceive before, the critical voice in your head, a slight squeal of feedback, or even a split-second eye contact with someone in the room.

Many of my students who send me videos for review are shocked at how nervous they get in front of a camera, even with no one else in the room! The "idea" of the camera rattles their stage-three achievement.

In stage four, distractions do still exist. It's not that they go away, or that you get Zen superpowers to overcome them.

What happens is that through strengthening your neural pathways, your body and unconscious memory can kick in and make corrections before your conscious mind does.

In stage four you are wired with the information, not just thinking it.

I can't tell you how many times onstage I thought, "Oh no, what's the next section?" and my hands simply went there, no problem, and played the music, thereby bailing me out.

That's stage four.

Let's take a look at the best practice strategy you can use to get your music to stage four.

Putting in time versus looking for results

I've already touched on this in the chapter about goal-setting, but it's something I learned from my teacher about practicing. It's worth going over this in detail so you can see how it applies in the practice room.

The best way to practice is to simply put the time in and not look for results. Looking for results when you practice is a recipe for frustration. Trust me, I know, as this is a trap I still fall into sometimes.

We are not used to being patient. We live in a society that gives us unnaturally immediate results. We order on Amazon and get next-day delivery. We buy an app and have it on our phone in seconds. We post on social media and get a dopamine hit within seconds when someone "likes" it.

The immediate gratification is not what nature intended.

Nature works more slowly, as does our musical development. So while our intellect may grasp an idea in seconds, it can take weeks, months, even years for our minds and bodies to show mastery of those concepts.

And that's totally okay.

Looking for results is like looking at the grass every hour to see if it's grown. It has surely grown, but the growth may be so imperceptible that it feels as if it has not grown.

A better way to measure progress is by checking that you regularly "put the time in." That way you measure your performance, rather than results.

This attitude enables you to show up and simply get to work, even if things feel weird, or sound wrong for a little while.

It also helps if you understand that it's okay to finish your practice session and leave things in an unfinished state. You know that you'll come back tomorrow and put some more time in.

I try to never end a practice session feeling defeated. If a project is under construction, it's okay for it to be unfinished.

I try to use this attitude with any project I take on, musical or otherwise. Heck, the book you are reading was not written in one sitting! I had to commit to repeatedly showing up and writing.

Make it easy to get started

You'll practice more consistently if you make it easy for yourself to get started. When there's a hurdle to getting started with anything, the less likely we are to do that thing.

One of the top reasons people sign up for fitness club memberships but don't go is because it's a hassle to get there.

Once we get started, it's easy to get into a flow. For example, once people actually get to the fitness studio, the workout session happens by itself.

Getting started is the hardest part. After that, it's easy.

For that reason, I suggest you find easy ways to get started practicing.

I have a few tricks I use so I can easily get started:

- I have guitars out on stands so they are easy to just pick up and play.

- I schedule small blocks of time, just to get the guitar in my hands.

- If my goal is simply to get the guitar in my hands, I know a longer practice session will usually unfold.

Case study: my mom and her iPad

Here's a cute and true story about my dear old mom, God rest her soul.

She wanted to get up-to-date with technology, so she got herself an Apple iPad.

However, she had a very old-fashioned mentality about using it.

She kept it turned off so as not to waste electricity, and kept it packed in the original box for safe keeping, which in turn was tucked away in her work room, forty feet away from the kitchen table, where she sat all day.

I kept telling her to just leave it turned on and have it on her kitchen table because I saw she'd never use it her way. But no, she knew better.

As you can imagine, using the iPad was a total pain in the neck for her. Unpacking it and powering it on was an "event." The entire thing felt like a project to her.

When she did try to use it, she had to learn from square one each time how to locate and start the email app.

Next she had to figure out where the compose-, send-, and receive-buttons were, and so on. It stressed her, and it was unenjoyable.

She simply didn't use the iPad enough to remember how to use it. It became such a drag for her that she was happier leaving it in the box.

The moral of the story? Have your instrument and environment set up in such a way that you can get started easily and quickly.

Consistent practice versus dabbling

Abe Lemons observed: "One day of practice is like one day of clean living. It doesn't do you any good."

I'll admit it, there are areas in which I dabble. I go through phases where I'll poke around at a piano, play some electric bass, and hey—it's fun. It informs my music, but because I don't stick with it regularly, I don't really improve much.

That's dabbling.

A dabbler stops doing something the minute it's no longer "fun." A dabbler doesn't *really* want to accomplish anything deep, because it's not "fun" to do the work.

Practicing guitar, on the other hand, is something I've dedicated to on a lifelong basis. I know that the only way to "move the needle" is to keep coming back, day after day, even if I feel no change or improvement.

My attitude is: "I practice when I feel like it, and *I practice when I don't feel like it.*"

On the days that I don't feel particularly inspired, I don't think about it too much. I just get the guitar in my hands and make sure I've made it easy for me to get started.

Environment is key

Your environment is an essential factor in your ability to build a consistent practice routine.

Sometimes we mistakenly think we need more discipline, when in fact what we really need is the right environment. The right environment will support the discipline.

You'll need an environment where you can practice and concentrate without any distractions. When you play there, no one else should be able to hear you. You need total solitude.

Many of us grew up in a household where there was a piano in the living room and everyone in the house would hear the person practicing.

The problem with practicing in front of others is there's always a level of self-awareness. If someone is listening, you might feel guilty if you need to practice something repetitive, or if you make mistakes.

In true practice, you need the freedom to make ugly sounds, try new things, play something over and over, fumble and fail. If you are glossing over the repetition that you need, in order not bore a family member who is listening, then your practice environment is not serving you.

It is for that reason I suggest you find a place in your home where you can practice without distraction and a place where no one else hears you.

Finding a practice space

Guitars are usually quiet enough to play at home. And while a living room may be comfortable and feel cozy, you may make better progress by setting up a music room in your basement where no one can hear you.

I can't tell you how many of my students come to concerts beaming and say, "I've been practicing your arrangement of 'In

My Life' for months," and their wife or girlfriend adds, "Yeah, and I never want to hear it again!"

That's a terrible pressure to deal with when you know that somehow the people closest to you are somehow not digging it. When your family (especially your partner) does not support you, it can psychologically undermine your sincerest efforts in accomplishing anything.

Do yourself, your music, and your family a favor, and find a dedicated practice environment.

Take breaks when you practice

It is physically and mentally critical to take breaks when you practice.

There is a super technique called the "Pomodoro Technique" that I loosely follow.

The Pomodoro Technique is basically as follows:

- Using a timer, work/practice/study for twenty-five minutes.

- Take a break for ten minutes.

- Do three or four rounds like this.

I am much more casual about it, but the idea is the same. I practice for roughly twenty to twenty-five minutes and then take a break. Then, I go back for another round.

Incredible things happen when you take breaks.

First, the brain tends to retain what you worked on at the start and end of your practice session. So, breaks will help you solidify images, sounds, and ideas.

Plus, during breaks, the subconscious mind will still continue to solve problems it had been working on.

So go ahead and take a break… place that phone call, make a cup of coffee, and pet the cat! Your subconscious mind is hard at work, sorting out the musical issues you were just working on.

Many times I've come back after a break in a video session and had an "aha" guitar moment. It's usually after the break that I've gotten the perfect video take after struggling in the taping session before the break.

Plus, physically, you need breaks. Your body is not built to do a singular motion over and over for hours, whether it's driving, sitting at a desk, or playing a guitar.

Blood has to flow, and all parts of the body and the body as a unit need to move. Moving your body when you take breaks will help your mind stay sharp and creative.

The takeaway

Let's do a quick chapter review:

- *Remember the four stages of learning.* For performance you need to be in stage four, which is unconscious competence. That's where you can roll out of bed and play the piece of music, because you have it wired into your system.

- *Put in the time, and don't look for results.* Keep doing your practice work patiently, and congratulating yourself on showing up. Results come later.

- *Make getting started easy.* Once you are started, it's easy to keep going, but getting started is the hardest part.

- *Consistent work beats dabbling.* Dabblers stop when the work is no longer fun. They can be very talented people. Just keep showing up to practice—it will pay off! If it feels un-sexy, you are probably going in the right direction.

- *Establish your practice environment.* Regardless of your talent, your environment can either support or hinder you. Find a dedicated space where no one can disturb you or hear you.

- *Take breaks when you practice.* Your body and mind need breaks, and your subconscious will work on problems during breaks. You'll come back with "aha" moments after breaks, I promise!

Chapter Seven

How to Get Out of a Practice Rut

"Trust the process. Your time is coming. Just do the work and the results will handle themselves."

~ Tony Gaskins

OFTEN STUDENTS WILL reach out to me and say, "I'm in a rut!"

What is a rut?

A rut is when you feel stuck because you are playing the same things and getting the same results. You yearn for something new and exciting, but you can't seem to think of anything, and you end up going in circles.

Nothing feels fresh, everything feels stale, and you see no way out of the spin cycle you are in. It's that hamster in-the-wheel feeling of running but not getting anywhere. Even though you are working hard at your guitar playing, nothing noticeably new is happening in your playing, and it's just not fun.

I know this feeling very well. It sucks. (You'll learn however, that it is a necessary and natural part of the learning process.)

Let's look first at why we feel disappointed. It has something to do with brain chemistry.

We all have a chemical in our brains called *dopamine*. When dopamine is released into our system, we feel good.

Because it feels so good, we can get addicted to the things which trigger it's release. Consequently, if we don't get the dopamine "kick" that we crave, we may end up feeling disappointed, discouraged and depressed.

Here's a short list of **healthy** stuff that can trigger a release of the feel-good chemical, dopamine.

- Love and approval from others
- Loving others
- Falling in love
- Loving and caring for your pets
- Being needed by others
- Audience approval, (applause, cheering, appreciation)
- Earning Money
- Spending money
- Making a discovery
- Accomplishing a goal
- Exercise
- Traveling somewhere new

In moderation, all of these things are totally ok.

Here's a musical list of things that may trigger a dopamine release:

- Hearing great new music for the first time
- A listener or audience loving your music
- Trying out a new guitar
- Getting a new piece of musical equipment
- Feeling good about your guitar playing
- Signing up for music lessons
- Getting hired for a performance
- Learning something new on guitar

As you can see, all of these triggers are harmless and actually pretty good for you. They make life worth living!

But here's the catch - the more and more a trigger is used for a dopamine release, the less sensitive you become to it (and the more you crave it, and look for it.)

Some examples of becoming de-sensitized may be:

- You hear piece of music the first time, and you get goosebumps or even cry - but after 100 listens, it loses its emotional effect on you.

- You taste that first spoon of chocolate ice cream and it's amazing, but after 2 bowls of ice cream you don't feel that same "kick" you felt with the first spoonful.

- You buy a new guitar and it's the most gorgeous, best sounding guitar you've ever played and feels incredible in your hands; after years you still love it but it's become more normal and does not feel as new as it did on day one.

- You learn a new song or "lick" on the guitar and you are filled with inspiration; after years, it's part of your playing but you don't feel the same inspiration you did when the information was new.

When you become de-sensitized to a trigger, it can lead to a feeling of disappointment because you are simply not getting the dopamine kick.

Now can you see what's happening when you are in a guitar "rut"?

You're de-sensitized because you have been playing the same stuff over and over, and you are not getting your dopamine kick from your own guitar playing.

How can we deal with this in a healthy and productive way?

Short-term solution: the quick fix

Think of this as a musical "Snickers bar." It's not the ultimate, long-term solution and should not be your main "source of nourishment," but it can make things more fun for the moment.

Do a quick change-up on yourself. Try something like:

- Playing a different guitar from the one you have been playing
- Fool around with some effects pedals
- If none of these are handy, go to a music store and try stuff out
- Fool around on another instrument, like a piano, bass, or mandolin
- Jam along with a recording just for fun

- Jam with others, including new musicians *(highly recommended)*
- Play something with a capo at a new fret
- Take a lesson
- Learn a new song

These activities will help you get back to the feeling of playing being fresh and fun, which will be a little ray of sunshine in your current grey, cloudy "stuck" feeling.

A personal example

Recently I got myself an electric bass, exactly for this reason. I needed something I could pick up that was just different, that would set off new little reactions in my brain. This wasn't for an audience—it was just for me.

Jamming on the bass got me to feel, see, and hear new things. New musical thought processes started. That made me think about some different guitar techniques and opened up some cool, new ideas.

Coming back to my main guitar routine, I did not feel quite as stuck as I did previously. I needed the fresh air that this little change-up brought.

In moderation, the short-term fix is okay!

A little lift is a good thing, the same way a little chocolate ice cream can be a good thing.

The danger of the short-term fix is that if that's all you

do, it's like always starting something from square one. That's dabbling.

There's a place for dabbling. It's totally okay. I do it from time to time.

Just know that you'll never get that really deep, satisfying feeling of accomplishment from dabbling.

Long-term solution: understanding plateaus

For my money, this is a better way to see, understand, and deal with the stuck, "I'm in a rut" feeling.

There's a common misunderstanding regarding how we make musical progress.

Progress is not a steady climb of noticeable improvement. Rather, it shows up as a sudden leap of realization to a new level after hanging out on a plateau for quite some time.

When you experience a plateau, it feels as if nothing is changing even though there is consistent effort. Under the surface however, thoughts are reorganizing, and the subconscious mind is preparing itself for the jump to the next level.

Sometimes long, arduous periods of work seem hopeless, with no end in sight. It feels like a day-in, day-out grind. That's a rut.

But suddenly, an unexpected "aha" moment occurs, and our awareness, understanding, and technique can take a fast quantum leap up. Then we find ourselves on a new plane of understanding, a new plateau. We'll probably be there for a while as we digest what that new level has to offer.

The same can be seen in nature. Winter always seems like

an endless stretch of dark and cold. Then one day those first buds come on the trees, and the little, purple, flower blossoms are just "there" suddenly. Spring is here, and we hadn't even seen it coming. The change is not gradual, it's "overnight." But in reality, it was brewing in the background all along.

Your next evolutionary leap

You may *feel* like you are stuck, when in fact you may be exhausting the possibilities and testing the boundaries of your current plateau. When the time is right, something in you will see a new possibility. This may come in the form of a new curiosity, or it may come as an "aha," "of course," or "d'oh" moment.

But there's a price to pay for the "aha" moment. You'll have to go through the plateau, and ride it out. Just keep putting the time in.

What does musical evolution feel like?

It's not actually that you conquer the thing you feel you are up against.

It's more like the universe hears your sincere efforts and is testing you. It asks you "How hard are you willing to work? How patient can you be?"

Then, through grace, you see a possibility that you had not previously seen. It was there, waiting for you in plain view, only you were not ready for it until now.

You start to play with this new possibility or viewpoint, and a small feeling of "yes" grows inside you. You know you're onto something.

You find yourself smiling and enjoying your new solution. It had been there the whole time, but you couldn't see it until you looked everywhere, tried everything, and eventually surrendered.

Bingo! *You evolved.*

The takeaway

Learning is not a steady climb. You will have alternating cycles of leaps in awareness and plateaus where things appear not to change at all.

Sometimes, during the plateaus, you may feel like you're in a rut.

There are two ways to handle the feeling of being in a rut.

1. *Do a short-term reset.* This can get things flowing again. Play a new guitar, listen to something new, maybe jam with some other musicians.

2. *Ride out the plateaus.* This requires a longer-term perspective, but sometimes one just has to be patient and not force things. As you feel you are covering the same ground, your body is digesting new sensations and you are rewiring your system. Your next evolutionary leap will come when it's time.

Chapter Eight

Building a Great Practice Routine

"When I was young, I never wanted to leave the court until I got things exactly correct. My dream was to become a pro."

~ Larry Bird

IT'S IMPORTANT TO understand that there are different types of guitar practice you will do. You may touch on a few of these in a single practice session.

Some different types of practice are:

- *Learning new concepts* – This can happen even without a guitar in your hands, and it greatly informs your playing. Examples would be the study of harmony or rhythm.

- *Technical Inquiry* – Maybe you're watching your hands,

listening to your tone, and seeing that everything feels good as you play. You're making small adjustments, trying new fingerings, and so on.

- *Warming up* – This can be light, easy exercises that ease you into playing guitar. It's best to have a routine.

- *Rhythmic warm-up* – Playing the mother rhythm on a hand drum to activate the sound and vibration within your touch and tone.

- *New tunes* – This could encompass any of the four stages of learning a new song.

- *Preparing for a gig* – You can do an alternation of new tune/old tune. This keeps your repertoire in balance.

- *Creativity* – When creativity strikes, and you get a brilliant idea for a song or an arrangement, just give it your attention so you don't lose the moment. Don't worry about maintaining a practice routine when this happens. When creativity strikes, go with it!

My practice routine

My practice routine generally has two parts, and this structure may or may not be appropriate for you. I'm just including it here so if you're curious, that way you'll know what I do.

My practice routine part one: warm-up

I spend fifteen to twenty-five minutes on part one of my warm-up. I usually begin with my groove-scales exercise (available as a free download at http://adamrafferty.com/lessons). If it's not this warm-up, it's another. The point is, I do something very gentle to loosen up and wake up my musicality.

This exercise is simply major and minor scales up and down the instrument—*but* played with a "walking bass line" groove. I play this slowly with a "pocket," so it's music, not just an exercise.

This helps me wake up hands and musicality. I have to instantly integrate my sense of tone, touch, and groove from the start.

In this exercise I repeatedly go from the lowest notes of the guitar to the highest, so the volume and tone in each register is as optimal as I can get it.

My practice routine part two: music repertoire/creativity

I review my old tunes often. Very often. Maybe too often.

I'll start a repertoire practice session with an old tune that allows me to listen to the guitar and music as a whole. I think of this like I'm a soundman listening to the first sounds of a band through a PA system. I'll ask myself, "Do I hear the melody? Do I hear the bass? It is grooving?" I'll then massage the sound in the direction needed.

Then I'll either work on a new tune, or I'll pull out an old tune and scan for trouble spots and see if I can make improvements.

Even on tunes I think I know, there will always be small mistakes if I have not played them in a while, so review is important.

If I'm developing a new playing technique, I may have to get old tunes to work with my newer concept.

For example, I recently discovered a new way to play a few bass notes so they "sit in the pocket" better on Stevie Wonder's "Higher Ground." It was an issue that had bugged me for years, and an answer showed up just two days before writing this.

Today's work will be recording that technique on my voice-memo app, listening to make sure it sounds okay, and then practicing it so my hands do it automatically (stage four) without my brain thinking about it (stage three).

Creative practice

When a new creative idea comes knocking, I drop *everything* and flesh out the invention. This could be a new song, an arrangement idea, or even improvising.

I have found that if I get a creative impulse but put it off "until later," the idea is never quite the same, or as fresh. I think I probably missed out on a few great tunes due to that. So, strike while the iron is hot, as they say.

I think of it as a very special guest showing up spontaneously at my home. I have to drop whatever my planned routine is because of this special event.

What about warming up for a concert?

I'm adding this here because it's *similar* to practicing.

When I warm up for a concert, I do things a tad differently from many other guitar players.

I always warm up backstage right until the moment I go on, but not nervously. I try to stay mellow and loose as I warm up, to save energy for the performance. Kind of like a baseball player warming up swinging a bat, gently. I never, ever go on stage "cold."

Sometimes at festivals, other colleagues or my students perform before me, and I feel like I "should" listen to them. But if I have to get onstage, playing well for the audience is my number-one goal, so I have to stay focused. For me that means warming up until show time and not watching the other performers.

Just last night I was practicing in the men's room at a small theater before I went on, as there was no proper backstage, and I needed to be alone so I could get into my groove. (There's a filthy joke in here somewhere...)

Many guitarists just try to play fast tempos backstage to make sure their "chops" are fired up and ready. But that's very one-dimensional. I used to do that, but I found I'd get very fatigued before I went on.

A better approach is to be groovy and loose instead of tight and fast. Always remember, power wins over force.

A few hours before the gig, I'll play the drum to really get my body rhythm, touch, and tone all wired together. Sometimes I'll even play the drum in my dressing room backstage.

Backstage I will play some groove tunes, and simply scan for touch and tone rather than technical perfection.

Then I will play at least one ballad like "Imagine" to activate the lyrical side of my playing, and listen intently to the sound of the guitar.

Then I am ready. Show time!

Onstage, it's time to flow, and everything must come from

the place of stage four. I commit to a right-brain approach to communicate flow, groove, and tone to the people.

Warning: If backstage you are feeling insecure as to whether you'll remember something onstage, that's a sure sign it is not in stage four. So just play something you know well, instead. I don't want you to poop your pants. You'll know when a new song is ready for its first performance.

Throwing technique away (well, not really)

When I am in part one of warm-up, I allow my left brain to think about technique, and hand position, and I may tinker with new ideas here.

It's like the laboratory where I allow myself to experiment.

For part two (music, repertoire, creativity), there are absolutely no technical exercises. Everything here is in the service of musical flow.

There is a famous expression among jazz musicians: "When the downbeat hits, B.S. walks."

This means that when you count your song in "1, 2, 3, 4," the next beat is the downbeat. At that point *nothing* matters except the music. No analytical thinking allowed after that point!

It's a good idea to practice like this as well, so you can simulate what will happen in a real-life playing situation.

The takeaway

It's important to understand that there are many different types of practice and areas of music to study.

They can be technique, warming up, studying new ideas, reviewing old repertoire, developing new repertoire, and creativity.

I suggest a basic framework of two parts. Part one is a warm-up to allow your body and musical soul to wake up.

Part two is the more musical aspect where you will play music with a flow, as best you can. Even if you have to go slow and play pieces in sections, you must feel what it is like to be in a flow so you'll be getting yourself ready for a performance.

PART THREE

YOUR LISTENERS

Chapter Nine

Getting Yourself Out There

"This idea of shared humanity and the connections that we make with one another—that's what, in fact, makes life worth living."

~ Clint Smith

YOU MAY BE playing music for yourself as a hobby, but the moment might come where you want to play some music for someone else. You may get an itch to perform at an open mic or at a friend's wedding or even do a full-fledged gig on your own. Or you may want to make an online video and share it with the world.

That's not surprising, because we are social beings, and music is a way to connect with others.

For me, the itch to perform is one that I have had my entire life. The musician in me loves the introvert part: the knowledge, the study, the theory, and the practice. But the extrovert/

performer part of me strives to connect with people and light up their souls with my guitar and "shtick."

Performing brings up a person's inner-game issues as well. You come face-to-face with insecurity, nerves, ego, and really seeing if your practice is, in fact, effective.

I'd also like to say: you don't have to perform! If you don't want to, that is certainly okay. My dad, for example, loves coming home and picking tunes on his guitar after a long day at work, and that's fine for him. He's not interested in playing for anyone other than himself and his three dogs.

But if you do feel that you'd like to maybe get on a stage and play guitar for an audience, I will try to give you some helpful information in the pages ahead.

One huge benefit of performing

One reason I recommend performing to students (and to you) is that you have no choice other than to get into a musical flow. Because performing has that effect, I find it to be therapeutic for me.

It's easy (for me) to get into a practice rut where "perfection and no mistakes" becomes the highest ideal. This mindset makes playing an activity where you find yourself practicing a piece over and over, with no real payoff.

But when you perform for people, you have to play the song and accept bumps along the way. You're tuned into other people's joy, and it's a nice break from being analytical and self-critical. You get to enjoy the fruits of your labor.

Being in a musical flow teaches, heals, and soothes the soul even if there are mistakes. You'll also find that many things you thought were mistakes were imperceptible to listeners.

At the end of the day, the challenge, excitement, and positive feedback you'll get from performing will invigorate your practice and give it new purpose.

Where can you perform?

A performance can be for a one-person audience or for a thousand people. Believe it or not, the concentration is the same whether it's for one or a thousand: you have to be 100% focused.

Sometimes smaller audiences can even make you feel more nervous, because it's more intimate.

Whether you're just starting out or you're a pro or semi-pro player, here are my ideas about how to find opportunities to perform.

Open mic sessions

One of the first places that musicians look to perform is "open mics" or "open stages." I think that's because there's a low price of entry. All one has to do is show up and sign up on the list, and bang! You are in.

However, this would *not* be my first recommendation for you to develop your performance.

Open mics can be very nerve-racking for performers, even though everything looks so casual and fun to outsiders.

The reason I'm pointing this out is so you don't blame yourself or avoid performing because of problems due to the open-mic environment.

Problems you may encounter at open mics

- *No backstage* – That means you have nowhere to warm up, plus maybe you feel obliged to listen to others. In the real concert world, one always has a backstage room and walks onstage ready, after a nice warm-up.

  Solution: If you're ever in this situation, go find a stairwell, a restroom, an office, or anywhere else to warm up. You need not sit in the audience the whole time and wait your turn.

  Be sure to warm up first at home so that the music is flowing, then do a quick one again before going onstage.

  Never, ever, ever go onstage without warming up a few minutes before. You are not obliged to listen to the other performers. You are there to play.

- *No sound check* – On a gig where you or your band is the main act, you'll get to set up your own gear and have a sound check with an experienced soundman so that you can get an ideal sound in the house, and onstage as well. At open mics, you may suddenly be hearing yourself loud through a stage monitor, or have your instrument feedback, and this can throw your game.

  Solution: With experience you'll learn how to accept and handle these situations. Just don't blame yourself. I'd say, play an easy piece as you start out so you can be on autopilot while you assess the sound situation.

- *Too short a time slot* – Often by the time you've played two or three tunes, your jitters calm down, and you're feeling more confident. Then you really feel ready to play, but at open mics, that's when you have to get offstage. In a real-life concert situation, that may be the point where the music gets better and better.

Solution: Put the open mic in context. Don't look to open mics for musical and performance satisfaction. Look to them as an opportunity to connect with a musical community.

Above all, remember that they are often the most uncomfortable playing situations of all, even for pros!

Playing at church

I don't attend church, but I have many musician friends who play at church. Many churches have a band, stage, and soundman, and there is a musical director. Often the level of musicians is very good.

This may be a great opportunity to play, connect with musicians, and sort out your technical setup. You'll have to address things like how you amplify your guitar, set up your effects, and so on.

Plus, if you play solo guitar, maybe opportunities will arise in the service where you can perform a solo piece.

Small cafe gigs

I started my career as a jazz guitarist playing in cafes with a tip jar. Anytime I hear a cappuccino machine, I have flashbacks. Good ones!

I highly recommend a gig like this, especially if you play solo guitar and want to *ease* into performing.

Maybe there's a cafe or restaurant in your area where you can ask if you could do a one-to-two-hour gig at no cost to them. I don't encourage giving music away free forever, but this is just so you can get your feet wet playing live.

If you work during the week, maybe you can ask for a weekend brunch gig, maybe once or twice a month. Get creative.

Here are some of the benefits of a gig like this:

- *You can set up your own gear* – It's more relaxed all around this way. You can experiment, and you'll learn what you need to have, to be pro.

- *You have to run through full tunes* – This gets you out of the practice mindset and into a flow of music. It will also solidify your song list. Week after week, you can play your standard songs, and slowly add new ones.

- *Remember, it's background music* – Depending on how you see things, this can be negative or positive. For a rock band, this would not be ideal, but for a solo guitar player or small group, it's great, in my opinion.

  You'll get to play several tunes and get feedback from people without the full pressure of a stage show, spotlights, and a captive audience. Plus, you can repeat songs (if you do it with enough of a time interval between them.)

  You have to come to terms with the fact that people may be chatting, but your music will live on a different frequency level than their voices, so you need not play loud. They will hear it, and some will let you know how much they love your music!

  Before I started touring as a solo guitar player, I did

thousands of background gigs, and often had a great time. And in New York City, many world-class players will still do gigs like this *incognito* just for fun. It's true!

- *You have time to settle in and get warmed up* – Unlike an open mic where you have to get offstage after two or three tunes, here you have a chance to sink into a relaxed way of playing, on your own terms.

- *You have to stay in the game* – I love this benefit. Let's say you had a long week and you don't feel like going to your brunch gig on the weekend.

Well, if you committed to it, you have to, whether you feel like it or not. This is a blessing, as you've set up some accountability. It's an appointment. This occasional pain in the neck will ultimately serve you and make you a more solid player.

Many times I've been in between concerts at home, working on other projects such as online teaching, and not in playing mode. All of a sudden, I'll glance at the calendar and say, "Uh-oh, I have to be onstage in five days," and that will force me to make playing the number-one priority again.

Having to show up and play actually whips me back into shape and keeps me in the game!

- *You'll reap rewards from regularity* – If your gig is two to four times a month, you will benefit greatly. By going through the motions often, your skills will get sharper and sharper.

When you only have one gig every few years, it's a huge event. Maybe you invite everyone you know and it's very emotional for you. It's a great milestone, but musically speaking, it's like going jogging, once. You won't get as much out of it as you would get from a regular gig.

Touring and concert-show-type gigs

Maybe you're already a pro or semi-pro player and you're interested in touring, or your own "club gigs." These are more of a showcase which features your playing.

Over the last several years I've had many guitar players ask me how I did it, how I got on tour internationally, and how I got over twenty-million YouTube clicks. (YouTube kick-started my touring by increasing my visibility.)

I will do my best to describe the process and tell you what worked for me.

How I got twenty-million YouTube views

Luck, period.

The same music, if I uploaded it now in 2019 (the time of my writing this) may not be as successful. 2008 to 2012 was a great time for uploaders. YouTube has changed, and is way more crowded.

There are zero guarantees that you'll be a star on YouTube, but I do suggest putting some music up there. Anyone who would hire you will want to see a video.

Plus, you'll get a nice boost when you get good comments. Don't take bad comments too seriously, as there are jerks out there.

Asking for gigs can be an uphill battle

Badgering club owners or managers to give you gigs is, in my opinion, not the right way to get them.

For years as a jazz guy, I tried this tactic. To build up a two-week European tour, I'd wake up at 5 every morning and call clubs for months (before email existed). For every "yes," I got hundreds of "no's" and a hundred unreturned calls.

Not a good use of time, and very disheartening. I was swimming upstream while the flow was going downstream.

Understand that many venues get up to a thousand requests a day, so your email or call or demo CD package will be just another voice in the already screaming crowd. In the era of CD's, they'd get unending piles of CD's every day in the mail.

Here is where there's some serious inner-game stuff at work...

If you find yourself ruminating with thoughts like "So-and-so plays there—why won't they give *me* a gig?" you are heading toward a negative downward spiral, so listen up.

This feeling is really just a desire for approval, more than wanting a gig. You want to get recognition that you are good enough to be invited there.

Danger, Will Robinson! It is precisely the sense of lack that repels the exact thing you want!

I remember as a teenager, anytime I'd get a crush on a girl it was like I sprayed on girl-repellant. Showing interest in a girl just made me seem more stalker-like and weird to them.

Magically, the minute I lost interest, the same girls would

become interested in me. (I guess they wanted to make sure they hadn't lost their magic charms!)

So here's an area where you may be able to experience some inner growth. Scan your feelings with utter honesty. If you're feeling a needy sense of lack, others will sense it in your speech, actions, and body language. It might repel gigs, just the way I repelled girls at age fifteen.

The more easygoing you are about it and the less you care, the more abundant the scene will seem. It'll be as if opportunities are presenting themselves to you at every turn.

The best way to get gigs and performance opportunities

Drum roll please… *Make music that people like!*

That starts with all the practice and knowledge information in this book.

It's very un-sexy to be told that your practicing will help get you gigs, but it's true.

If you make good music that people enjoy:

- That lady hearing you at the cafe might ask you to play her daughter's wedding.

- That kid asks if he can take lessons from you.

- The other guitarists in town appreciate you and occasionally ask you to fill in for them.

- Your videos will get shared by the few who see them and dig them.

So, through practice and honing your craft, opportunities

will show up by themselves. And your success will never play out the way you imagine it should.

The practice room is where it all starts. Not on social media. Not with connections. Not by paying for promotion. Not with a thousand phone calls. Not by hanging out with the right clique. Those are simply add-ons.

Just practice. Learn. Take your craft seriously. Take lessons.

Good music will cut through all the B.S. like a knife.

Remember, try to have your finger on the pulse of what folks might like. Think: *what's in it for them?*

By thinking about your audience, you'll start to invert the process. Instead of thinking about *your* music and *your* gigs, you'll find people asking you to play, because they know something wonderful is in it for *them.*

In Chapter Eleven I'll show you some techniques I've used to connect with my audience and invert the gig-getting process so that people ask me to perform, rather than me asking them.

Some down-to-earth, quick, pro tips

If you are just starting out, here are some very basic ideas to help you any time you want to perform better. These will help you be more desirable to an audience, even if they don't realize what you are doing.

- *Tune up!* – I can't tell you how many guitar players or singer/songwriters get up on stage and have what would have been a great performance, only their guitar is out of tune, making it painful to listen.

  Get a decent, clip-on, digital tuner, and tune, tune,

tune. Get to know your guitar at home for all the micro-measurements in tuning.

Note: If you tune open strings, then put a capo on, *you must retune* with the capo on!

Plan to do your last fine-tune-up onstage.

If you can set up guitar pedals, they make tuning pedals that mute the sound so your guitar signal won't come through the PA system as you tune.

- *Warm up your voice* – If you sing, take some vocal lessons and learn a proper warm-up technique. This will make your vocal performance sound 99% better!

- *Check your gear at home* – Plug everything in at home a week before you perform. Surprises like crackly guitar input jacks, buzzes, and bad cables onstage can be avoided and addressed by your local repair person. If it's been a while since you plugged the guitar in, there may be oxidation in the input jack, for example.

  Also, you may be surprised to find out your guitar pickup makes everything sound and feel different.

  Play at home amplified so you can become friends with the plugged-in sound of your guitar.

  If you don't do this, the surprise of the new sound will make you very nervous! So go ahead and address this before you get onstage.

- *Bring a gig survival kit* – Bring at least one extra guitar cable more than what you think you need; bring extra strings and a peg-winder. Depending on the gig, you may even want to bring a backup guitar. It may seem extreme, but I always travel with two guitars.

- *Dress decently* – You need not dress formally, but decently. I learned this in my twenties. When you look good, people will take you more seriously and see you in a different light. If you're looking to get more performance opportunities playing guitar, *your shined shoes may matter more than you know!*

- I have a zero-decision "fingerstyle-guitar outfit" I wear so I don't need to think. Black shirt, jeans, polished shoes, and my cap. I never ever have to think about what to wear.

The takeaway

Not everyone is a performer. You may be an at-home hobby player, and that's totally fine. Really!

But if you're like me, you may get the itch to perform. There are many benefits to performing:

- You'll have to run pieces start to finish.

- You'll connect socially with your music.

- You'll get fresh motivation to keep going with practicing.

- You'll "stay in the game" and be accountable.

When it comes to places to perform:

- Be cautious at open mics or open stages. They look comfy but have lots of built-in problems.

- Find a small regular cafe or restaurant gig even if it's for free. That will help you sharpen your skills on many levels.

- If you're looking to do showcase gigs or tour, make

great music and allow the rest to follow. Don't go crazy trying to "make things happen."

Once you get the gig, it's all about showing up and doing your best. This is where stage fright and your inner critic can step in. Let's look at some inner-game tactics to battle these small demons.

Chapter Ten

Perfectionism, the Inner Critic, and Stage Fright

"Don't aim for perfection. Aim for 'better than yesterday'."

~ Izey Victoria Odiase

NERVOUSNESS, FEAR, AND stage fright sneak up on us from nowhere. At home when we play the guitar, everything seems perfect. But when we get up in front of people, uninvited fears arrive and can make playing a song a nerve-wracking, nightmarish experience.

Getting up onstage is like turning on a high flame inside our psyche. It often brings up deeply buried survival fears, even though it's just music. Our hands might involuntarily shake, heart rates increase, and a critical inner dialogue begin.

This is due to our good old *amygdala* (or reptilian brain) at work. When we sense an unknown situation or territory, it's that millions-of-years-old, primitive portion of our brain that tells us, "Get outta here before you get killed!" We enter fight-or-flight mode.

So when we get onstage to play music, the fear of death can literally kick in.

"Stage fright is my worst problem," says Andrea Bocelli, the famous Italian opera singer and songwriter.

In addition to the physical fear aspect, an unwanted voice sometimes enters: the voice of the inner critic. This is a voice that runs on its own, saying many of our buried, negative, psychological messages, commenting on our playing in real time.

So it's not us against the audience: it's us against ourselves. There is a degree of self-mastery to be achieved in this situation.

For the first five years I toured playing solo guitar, I would literally sweat through my shirts because of fear and nerves, yet I knew this was something I wanted to conquer. I literally had moments of nausea backstage before going on, where I thought, "This is my dream? Why the hell am I doing this to myself?"

The good news is that there are active steps you can take to help conquer these fears. I did, and you can too.

It's a spiritual journey

I see the overcoming of nerves and stage fright as a form of spiritual practice.

Mindfulness meditation practices teach us to focus on breath, observe our thoughts as they pass through, and come back to the breath.

Silently witness your thoughts as they arise, and don't

identify with them. Eventually they fade, and maybe new thoughts arise. That's all okay.

Meditation is not a "checking out" into a dream, fantasy, or sleep state as many people think. It's not a place to search for "groovy experiences" either.

A Buddhist version of meditation, called *mindfulness meditation*, is the practice of allowing everything to be as it is. You allow thoughts to come up, acknowledge them, and allow them to pass through. Observe them just as you would observe clouds floating through the sky.

I recommend a meditation practice for everyone. Done properly, it's the best stuff in the world. You don't have to get a guru or join a religion. Think of it the same way you need sleep or exercise. It's just plain good for you.

Even just ten minutes of sitting and breathing, allowing the mind to go crazy and *witnessing it*, can train you. It's exactly the skill you need to be the boss of your brain onstage.

When you first try to sit still and breathe, you'll see that you can't control your thoughts. That means it's working! Ideas about work, family, cleaning, and any other pressures will arise whether you want them there or not. Don't try to silence them; just let them float in and out. That's how mindfulness meditation works.

This will build your ability to be "the witness." If you can calmly witness what your mind is doing when you perform, that's 90% of the battle.

The trap of perfectionism

Striving to be excellent is noble, but perfectionism can be debilitating. I know this from firsthand experience. Perfectionists stop themselves before they even get started and barely ever finish anything. This is a terrible trap.

It is far better to get things done, to deliver, hit "publish," get on that stage, or whatever, and to get your forward flow going, warts and all.

Perfectionism distracts from the real work. In perfectionism lies ego, the thought of an "I" doing the work, and if you have any self-esteem issues (many of us do), it can just seem like it's never good enough.

Examples of perfectionism:

- You're building a website and you get stuck on choosing just the right background color, and you end up never finishing the site or launching.

- You're making a CD, and you record, mix, and edit much too long, and end up taking years to publish it, if ever. The entire project loses its freshness.

- You hold off getting onstage until you think you can play something perfectly (which will never happen.)

- You constantly mess with your fingernails instead of playing guitar (that's why I play no-nails!)

What are mistakes?

As musicians, we perceive mistakes as any kind of unwanted or unexpected bump or error in the music: a missed note, a forgotten passage, a botched place in the song.

Instead of hearing this tiny moment as part of the overall flow, we give it a disproportionately huge amount of importance. Sometimes the memory of having made a mistake can overshadow the remaining performance of a song. While everyone is enjoying the song, we're still obsessing about a mistake long gone by!

This tiny mistake can trigger the inner critic, negative self-talk, fear, and self-disapproval.

If I were to tell you to just "feel differently," that wouldn't change much. You will never, ever play the way your inner perfectionist wants perfection to sound.

Your inner perfectionist is on high alert for anything even slightly wrong.

So rather than addressing your feelings, let me give you some knowledge. This will help you see that "no-mistakes perfection" is simply the wrong target to aim at in performance.

The audience's perception versus your perception

Imagine that you have something stuck between your teeth. It consumes your full awareness and "is" your world. For outsiders, they have no idea of the thing between your teeth. It is nonexistent for them.

Little musical mistakes are just like that. No one knows or cares!

Another analogy is bike riding. When you're on a bicycle, you hit the little pebbles and bumps, and occasionally a bigger bump here and there. Plus, you're making thousands of small steering corrections to stay balanced. You actually are *not* moving forward in a straight line, but to an observer, you *appear* to be. They don't see the bumps or the steering corrections. They see you smoothly gliding forward on your bike.

I was on tour just last week, and an audience member commented, "Wow, you played perfectly, not one mistake!" I'm always honest and usually smile and answer, "Fooled you! I made about ten-thousand mistakes."

What you perceive as mistakes are usually imperceptible to others.

What do audiences hear?

Audiences don't hear tiny bumps, but they do hear things that relate to the horizontal flow of the music, things like:

- Groove

- Melody

- Tone

- Intonation (is the instrument in tune?)

If you stay in the flow, you can really play some wrong stuff and 99% of the time, no one will even notice. If you get out of the flow (such as stopping and starting), the audience will perceive a mistake.

If you stop and start when you make mistakes in practice,

you are building a bad habit. Why? Because it will feel natural to stop and start, and then will feel *unnatural* onstage to stay in flow. This is why I recommend practicing playing straight through pieces "warts and all."

If you do experience real trouble spots, it's time to do a different mode of practice. Slow down, look at your fingerings, and try to find a new solution. You may have to go back to the drawing board on how you play a passage. Then, slowly see if you can get the new solution in a flow.

After each gig, I remember the trouble spots and address them the next day when I practice.

How should you listen to your own music?

My teacher Mike was a pianist, composer, and arranger and taught me *listening* on a very high level. Being around him changed the way I listened to music. In fact, music sounded different to me when I was in the room with him.

Whether it had to do with playing, grooving, composing, arranging, or counterpoint, he always stressed the importance of the flow of the music, and downplayed the importance of perfection and details.

When we recorded my second CD in New York City, I used one of his peers on the drums, a master drummer who played with just about everybody in the 60's and 70's.

Yet, at the session I felt dissatisfied with the way he played. I had some pre-conceived notions about how I wanted the drums to sound. (That was already a problem—I should have let him be who he was and trusted his expertise.)

Because of my ideas, the session ended up being extremely

tense. I wasn't happy, and he felt it. And he wasn't happy with a young twerp like me judging him. (I'm a middle-aged twerp now, but I was twenty-seven then.)

Later that week at my lesson, Mike and I listened to the rough CD tracks. I openly complained about the drummer's performance as the music played on the stereo.

That's when Mike did a Yoda on me. "What's your foot doing?" he asked, smiling.

Huh? My foot was tapping by itself—to the music. Busted!

He showed me that my ego idea of what "I" wanted, thought, had in mind, whatever, was overridden by the truth my body was telling me.

It grooved. My ego didn't want it to groove, but my foot told me it did.

"How bad could the drummer have played if your foot is tapping?" said Mike, smiling wryly.

Lesson learned. The old guys schooled the young guy, yet again.

That's the day I learned to focus on flow and not get too caught up on details. It's another dimension of listening. It's like a painter stepping back from the canvas to take in the whole, instead of getting caught up in the micro-details.

The funny thing is, the average person on the street listens to flow much more than many trained musicians do!

Now when I produce my own solo recordings or YouTube videos, I listen for what I learned about at that CD playback lesson. Sure, I'd love to play cleaner, but my main criteria is this: does it flow, can I hear the groove, and is the melody singing?

Naming your inner critic

If you start having a critical voice in your head, here is an effective technique to put it in its proper place: *name it.*

I named mine "Darth," from Darth Vader, but I envision a baby-sized, annoying Darth Vader.

When I start to feel self-destructive criticism churn up, I just say, "Oh, that's Darth." That helps me belittle it, compartmentalize it, shove it to the side, and get back on track musically.

I always get distracted when I play, but I have trained the ability to come back to my present moment by internally saying "come back."

The wisdom of 'keep smiling'

I have a story I'd like to share with you. This was one of the greatest guitar lessons I ever had.

In 2008 I had recorded a duo CD with a fabulous vocalist named Sabine Kühlich, and we set up a five-week tour in Germany to support the CD.

My solo concerts were on hold, as I was focused entirely on this duo project. But someone saw I was in their area and had a night off, so they offered me a concert.

"Sure!" I said. While I had been playing a lot, it was the duo repertoire. My solo repertoire was a tad rusty.

Sabine's uncle drove and helped me set up that night. He had a small camcorder and offered to videotape the concert.

As I botched one or two notes, my inner critic, Darth, kicked in: "See, you got lazy by playing duo! You haven't been practicing enough of your solo repertoire. The people are looking at you funny: they know! I don't know if you're really good enough for a solo career."

Then the following cycle kicked in:

- The more I listened to the critic, the more upset I got.

- The more upset I got, the less I smiled.

- The less I smiled, the weirder the audience felt.

- The weirder they felt, the less I smiled.

- The cycle spun downward, everyone felt weird, and I finished the gig.

That night, riding home in the car was mental agony. I was ready to quit. I felt I had failed miserably and just beat myself up no end.

The video revelation

The next morning, in hopes of punishing myself further, I decided to face the music and watch my "horrible" concert on video. Ah, delicious self-flagellation over coffee!

Here's how my self-dialogue went as I watched: "Well, the first song is fine—I always start with that. I know it will get worse. Second song… hmm, not so bad, but the mistakes happen later. Third song—aha, there was that mistake, but geez, it was not actually a big deal. Wow, I haven't been smiling a whole lot. Fourth song—it sounds okay, but gosh, I'm not looking too happy. Wow, the playing is actually okay. If I would have smiled more, the people would have been happier."

The big mistake was that I was not smiling. *The playing was fine.*

But this happened all because I took all the little bumps in the road way too seriously when I was performing. In turn, I lost sight of the big picture, which was *communication with the audience.*

Moral of the story? Don't take mistakes too seriously, stay with the flow, and keep smiling!

Take Deep Breaths

When we get stressed, we get a surge of cortisol and adrenaline. These hormones create a fight-or-flight response in the body.

An adrenaline rush was very useful to cavemen so they could feel fear and run away extra fast if they were being attacked by saber-toothed tigers, but it is not helpful to us as musicians who need control of fine, precise motor skills.

The fight-or-flight reaction sends blood away from the brain and out to the limbs, essentially making us dumber and stronger.

As guitarists, we don't want to play with a heavy, over-strengthened touch. That can cause us to squeeze the neck too hard and pluck the strings too heavily. We need to maintain a degree of control as we play. And we want to be mentally on point as well.

A few deep breaths can really calm the nerves. When we breathe deeply, we activate the parasympathetic nervous system, which helps switch off the fight-or-flight hormones. It also helps you bring focus inward and improves cognitive function.

A crazy but true stage-preparation story

I once read a story about how a group of Olympic gold medalists trained one year. They actually did mock competitions, like dress rehearsals, to really live the feeling of the pressure, and also did pretend "Gold Medal winning" to live the feeling of winning over and over again.

The crazy thing is, when they got to the real Olympic competition, they felt as if they'd been there before. They were not thrown by nerves, and felt the win was inevitable. Sure enough, they won.

When I read this, I decided to try the same technique for one of my first solo tours. I was pretty nervous about doing a complete concert and didn't want to come on tour "cold."

I decided to go "on tour" right inside my New York City apartment. I wanted to feel the nerves, the weak spots, and go through all the motions so I'd feel a little more prepared for stage.

I did the following, right in my apartment:

- Set up a small PA system
- Bought some inexpensive, colored, DJ spotlights to shine slightly in my face and make it feel like I was onstage
- Set a concert start time
- Made my kitchen into a "backstage"
- Set up a video camera to record, so it felt like someone was watching
- Made sure at the end to visualize the happy faces

Sure enough, I got as nervous as if I were onstage. I knew I was at home, but this made it feel totally different than sitting on my couch and playing.

This preparation actually helped a lot. I can remember getting on the tour, and just like the Olympic athletes, I felt as if I had recently been in a public performance!

Keep performing

All the words in this chapter are fine and good, but no words will ever amount to your real-life experience. You have to pass through these fires yourself, just as I did. I can only point the way for you.

- The more you perform, the less unknown it feels.

- The less unknown it feels, the safer you feel.

- The safer you feel, the less the reptilian brain kicks in.

- The less the reptilian brain kicks in, the more fun you have.

- The more you do it, the more confident you become.

The takeaway

Nerves, stage fright, perfectionism, and the inner critic are all basically a fear reaction. The reptilian brain interprets the fear as a life-or-death situation, and puts us into fight-or-flight mode.

When we're experiencing such feelings, it's impossible to think our way out.

One trick to overcoming this is to understand that what the audience perceives is not what we perceive.

Audiences perceive musical flow as groove, melody, and

sound. Keep an eye and ear on those aspects, and the music will sound good.

Also, keep smiling! You can *sound* awesome, but if you *look* unhappy, the audience will wonder what's bugging you.

In the next chapter, I'd like to show you some secrets of how to strengthen your relationship with your audience, and get invited to more places to perform, more often.

Chapter Eleven

Musical Communication with Your Listeners

"Music is the greatest communication in the world. Even if people don't understand the language that you're singing in, they still know good music when they hear it."

~ Lou Rawls

PRACTICING, LEARNING, AND honing your musical craft is one of the most intimate and soulful things you can do. In solitude, you meditate on what melody, rhythm, and harmony mean to you; you spend hours, weeks, even years working on your touch, tone, and technique.

While this is utterly personal, if you want to communicate with your listeners, you'll have to think about their experience as well.

- Will your music speak to them?

- Will it communicate the feeling you intend?

- How can you build your relationship with the audience?

- Can you maintain your musical integrity while pleasing the audience?

Double attention

In the martial arts, there is a concept called *double attention.*

Imagine you are on the street witnessing a beautiful, festive parade. Your wallet is in your back pocket.

- If you're only outward in your attention, watching the parade, a thief can easily take the wallet out of your pocket without your noticing.

- If you're only inward with your attention, making sure no one steals your wallet, you miss out on enjoying the lovely street parade.

- If you can keep your attention on both the parade and your wallet at the same time, you can enjoy the day and hang on to your wallet. That's what is meant by "double attention."

I recommend using the concept of double attention in your music, so that you can make music from the heart and still communicate with your audience effectively.

The artist and the entertainer

It's up to you to figure out the proper balance of being an artist versus being an entertainer. Sometimes they seem at odds with each other.

The *pure artist* goes deep into exploring and creating art and might not be concerned about reaching an audience at all. If there is an audience, it's up to them to decipher and understand her creations. The pure artist goes only with her inspiration, and has very little concern for commercial success.

The pure artist does not sugarcoat her art to make it easy for anyone to understand. The general public may find her art ugly, obscure, weird, and unenjoyable, and that's okay with her. For this reason, many pure artists have small audiences. To the pure artist, there is no other path, as anything other than this would feel like a sellout.

Examples:

- Modern classical music
- Free jazz
- Modern art
- Anything very avant-garde or disturbing

The *pure entertainer*, on the other hand, puts the audience's pleasure first. For him, it's not so much about what he does but how well he does it. The *delivery* of the show is all-important to the entertainer.

The general public can understand the pure entertainer easily. The pure entertainer makes sure to choose material that is enjoyable and does not require too much concentration or intellect. There is no heavy decoding work required of the audience to be entertained.

The pure entertainers have to hone a craft and practice, but their end goal is to communicate with the audience in an utterly enjoyable and easy-to-understand way.

Examples:

- Cover bands
- Magicians
- Comedians
- Circus acts
- Movies
- DJ's

Finding the sweet spot

For me personally, either of these "pure" extremes is undesirable. I seek a middle way and would encourage you to do the same. It's all about locating the sweet spot between these two positions—artist and entertainer—that suits you best.

For me, an avant-garde jazz group, playing completely "free jazz" with sound effects, no harmony, no rhythm, and no melody, is pure torture. It's not that I don't understand it. I understand it just fine, and I don't like it.

On the other hand, I find completely sugary, predictable, pop music simply nauseating. It's like cotton candy: there's just nothing there—no grit, no substance, nothing to make me think, nothing to challenge me.

I enjoy music which blends both art and entertainment.

For example, Stevie Wonder writes highly inventive music using jazz harmonies and interesting melodies, but also uses infectious grooves, catchy hooks, and great song structures.

Mozart is another great example; his tunes are easily singable for average listeners, but for musicians who listen more deeply, his genius is unparalleled.

Your sweet spot is the intersection of what you find interesting and what you think the audience will like. When that happens, it's a win-win.

How I started meeting the audience halfway

For years I played nothing but straight-ahead, bluesy jazz. I love that music, and I will always consider myself a jazz musician.

But there was a problem. Other *musicians* could understand what I was playing just fine, but the general public couldn't. To general audiences, my improvised jazz-guitar solos probably sounded like scrambled eggs.

I had a dream of touring and entertaining bigger audiences, yet it was very difficult to do so by playing "scrambled eggs" jazz guitar, because most audiences need music that's easier to understand.

So who was I playing for? The other musicians, or the audience? First, I had to answer this question honestly.

I'm not saying instrumental jazz can't reach a large audience. What I'm saying is, I had a burning desire to perform in a more extroverted way for more people. I was willing to reshape my musical message to achieve this aim.

Why do cover songs work?

I started noticing that anytime I played a tune people knew, they reacted more positively toward my guitar playing.

Why was this? Why did jazz go over their heads, but familiar tunes got their attention?

Aha! It's because they already had a picture in their mind of the tune, and could therefore *understand* what I was playing. They enjoyed that they were understanding it, and didn't have to work hard to decipher what they were hearing.

Think of going to an art museum. If you saw a completely abstract modern painting you might think, "Wow, it looks interesting," but you'd probably also feel "I don't actually get it."

Then, if you saw a portrait or a landscape painting, you'd probably find it much easier to appreciate the painter's skill, her sense of color, and her sense of shading because *you understand what you are looking at.*

I formulated this idea that was a total game changer for me:

C + Y = R

Cover Song + YOU = Relationship (with audience)

As soon as I started doing just a few familiar songs, it pulled people in. It was like magic. Better yet, I felt like a person dying of thirst in the desert finally getting a sip of water.

All the time I thought my problem was that my guitar playing wasn't good enough, and I finally got the message: "It's the tunes, stupid!"

I started getting more requests for concert appearances and lesson requests from students. In short, I inverted the entire process I had been doing before: instead of looking for an audience, the audience came looking for me.

I now work on a slightly different artistic angle than before. Instead of coming up with "genius noodly jazz guitar solos," I spend my energy crafting solo guitar arrangements with walking basslines, percussion, and a sparkling touch. I'm engaging artistically but putting my efforts in a different zone.

I still get to have my artistic integrity, but the understandable songs help build a relationship with the audience.

Ironically, when I mix in my original songs, someone usually says, "Wow, I really like your original songs. You should do more of them!"

The Beatles started as a cover band

The Beatles did not write "Twist and Shout"—they covered it!

Yes, you read that right!

One of the greatest songwriting bands of all time, the Beatles played cover songs in their early days to get audience "traction."

I glanced at Wikipedia the other day and saw a list of at least fifty songs the Beatles covered, including "Long, Tall Sally," "Roll Over, Beethoven," and "Twist and Shout."

"Twist and Shout" was actually first recorded two years earlier by a group called The Top Notes, then by The Isley Brothers, and then by The Beatles.

Singer-songwriters and cover songs

I've also seen how cover songs really help me as a listener when I attend shows of singer-songwriters.

Singer-songwriters pour their hearts, souls, and life stories into their songs. And it can be exhausting to listen to original songs for an hour. I feel their pain, but gosh, sometimes it all starts sounding the same.

One singer-songwriter friend once included a Marvin Gaye song in his set of otherwise original music. That one tune made my entire experience of his original music so much easier to take in! It offered relief from concentrating, and I could just kick back and enjoy the music, which is what I wanted to do on a Friday night.

I'm not suggesting that you sell out. What I'm saying is that if you'd like to have more chances to play live, find that sweet spot and meet the audience halfway. Stay open to covering one or two well-known songs that you love.

That may be just the thing to help you attract a larger audience. Hey, if it was okay for The Beatles, it's okay for you and me.

Some tips if you only play original music

If you want to play only original music, that's not only fine—it's noble and awesome! I support you 100%.

You don't "have to" play covers.

What I will suggest is that you think of ways to make your original music as enjoyable, memorable, and understandable as possible.

Here are some ways that come to mind:

Original music tip #1: make sure your songs have great hooks

Whether it's a solo guitar with no vocals, a jazz tune, a hip-hop song, or heavy metal, strive to compose songs or pieces with a memorable hook.

Here are two off-the-beaten-track examples: Merle Travis's "Cannonball Rag" has a memorable guitar hook, even though it's a solo fingerstyle guitar piece. Twisted Sister's "We're Not Gonna Take it" has a great vocal hook.

The one is Kentucky thumb-picking, and the other is glam metal. Neither of these songs is a favorite of mine, but gosh, those hooks are good! Regardless of style, you should have a great hook.

Mozart's "Eine Kleine Nachtmusik" is a world-class, genius-level, classical work, yet it still has a memorable pop-song-type hook that even the most uneducated listener could sing back after a single listening.

If your listeners tell you they can't stop humming your song, that means you have a good hook. Pop the champagne!

Does your music pass the melody test?

I suggest you hold your original music to the following test.

Can you sing the clearly defined melody away from your instrument?

If you can't, that's a sign that the song or composition itself might be weak.

No amount of gigging, fame, practicing, smoke machines, or studio mixing-tricks can make a non-song into a song, or make a bad song good. So always check to see if your music passes the melody test.

Modern guitar techniques

What about modern guitar techniques, like tapping, harmonics, effects, and using alternate tunings?

Well, I'm about to say something that will truly offend many fingerstyle guitar players, and I will make no bones about where I stand on this. Please hear me out.

Many players use modern and unconventional techniques such as:

- Percussion on the body of the guitar

- Right hand plays notes on fretboard

- Use of harmonics, maybe tapped by right hand

- Use of alternate tunings (although DADGAD is pretty much a standard tuning)

- Creative use of digital effects/reverbs/multiple pickups in guitar

- Looping pedals

All of these techniques and tools are *awesome*, and if they unleash creative ideas, that is 100% wonderful. If they are used to support a melody, you are good to go.

But here's where the danger lies. Many modern fingerstyle-guitar players get so enamored of the new technique or alternate tuning they're exploring, that they leave out melody. Oops!

You can use all these techniques, and yes, you can make a lovely, interesting soundscape. However, if you can't "sing the song," you didn't really compose anything: you simply experimented with cool yet meandering techniques, grooves, and sounds.

Hey, don't worry. When I was a kid, I did this, too. I can remember my days in college when I got involved in drum machines and recording-studio technology. I remember programming a cool beat and then writing a chord progression to it. I recorded synth keys and even added electric bass.

And then, all I had was a drumbeat with some R&B chords. The problem was that there was no song or melody as the basis of the music. I tried to improve it by messing with EQ, synth patches, and extra percussion, but it was simply "accompaniment in search of a song."

I wasn't just polishing a turd. I was rolling it in glitter dust.

Here are other examples of musical accompaniment in search of a song:

- Fingerpicking guitar chords (fast or slow, any style)
- Many house music/techno/lounge tracks
- Hip-hop beats
- Any kind of groovy percussion circle

All of these can offer an extremely nice temporary musical experience and may be suitable as background music in an elevator. But real musical compositions are based on melodic content, not effects.

So, can you sing the melody to your song or piece away from the instrument?

Original music tip #2: play with a groove

Great grooves will make your music infectious.

Grooves don't necessarily make music memorable, but they are important to keep your music flowing along. And if your audience is tapping their feet or even dancing, that's a beautiful thing!

In fact, just last week I saw a band called "Snarky Puppy," and they play a unique style of instrumental music that is sometimes very dissonant and complex, but *very* groovy.

There were jazzy melodies that I'm sure I could sing back if I listened to the music a few times. Irresistible melody wasn't the strongest point of the band. The groove and intensity were, and that was totally okay for a jazz festival.

The ability of listeners (like me) to swoon and groove to their music helped tie it all together and make the musical experience a good one.

How to build a great set list

Whether you're focused on original material, cover songs, or a mix of both, you will need to think about building a set list if you plan to play a thirty-to-sixty-minute set.

Here are a few tips to help you make an effective set list.

Set list tip #1: don't do too much of one thing

One slow love ballad can be beautiful; ten ballads will put people to sleep.

One fast number can fire up some great energy; ten fast tunes will wear people out and desensitize them.

One blues number is great. Ten blues songs will sound almost the same.

One percussive guitar song is groovy and neat to watch; ten are annoying and often lacking in melody.

One original singer-songwriter tune is a joy to listen to; ten songs in the same key with the same fingerpicking pattern sound the same, even if the lyrics are different.

Can you see where I'm going with this?

Set list tip #2: use different grooves throughout your set

People hear "feel" and tempos more than lyrics. How many varied feels do you have? I like to include these different grooves somewhere in each set. I think of them as colors:

- Funk
- Brazillian
- Ballad
- Folksong
- Swing
- Up-tempo

My "rule" is this: I never play two songs with the same feel and tempo back to back. I sculpt my sets as a journey of intensity and variation.

Set list tip #3: end the set with a bang

As you write your set list, think backwards from the *end* of your set.

What's the piece with the most powerful delivery that you have? How can you end the show with a BANG? *Consider that first!*

By providing listeners with a solid bang at the end, you cue them where to applaud, and they will appreciate your strength as a performer.

Set list tip #4: start your set strong

After deciding how you will end the set, think about how you will start it.

When you start, make your musical intention strong. It can be any type of tempo: a ballad, an up-tempo song, or anything in the middle. Just make sure you feel very sure about how you kick the tune off.

You may need to think about which of your songs is a good opener.

As you learn or compose new pieces, think of the colors, tempos, and flavors they provide. Changing feels and sounds during the set helps keep your audience engaged and awake.

Are you a giver or a taker?

All these ideas surrounding "artistic" versus "entertaining" serve a higher purpose. In my opinion, it's all about connecting with other human beings on a soul level through music.

Some musicians are givers and some are takers.

- *Takers* want to do their thing, and just be in their world. Their own enjoyment is the most important thing.

- *Givers* want to light up the hearts of their audiences. Audiences can feel the intention of such a performer.

The good news is that you can be an artist who enjoys their craft and also gives value to the audience.

I strive for my highest musical ideals, *and* I want my audience to have an utterly enjoyable time so they can experience a feeling of love and healing as a result of the music.

A priceless experience

A few years back, I played a concert in Milwaukee, and an old lady in a wheelchair approached me after the show.

"You had me dancing in my wheelchair!" she said. She was glowing. In what was probably a difficult and painful time for her, she felt joy that night.

You can't put a price on that. And I take no personal credit. I just let the music flow through me and am honored that I could serve up some happiness for her and others that evening. That's the real gig: the spiritual gig!

So that's why I pay attention to the artist/entertainer balance—C + Y = R—and putting enough variation in my set. So that old lady could dance in her chair and feel some joy and musical healing.

The takeaway

Maintain your integrity as an artist and reach for your highest ideals. Find the balance between artist and entertainer that best suits you.

At the same time, try to see if somehow you can meet your audience halfway while staying aligned with your integrity. It will be easier for them to enjoy what you have to offer, and you will feel honest about what you do.

By serving the audience, you become a giver as opposed to a taker. I'm sure you've heard the phrase "It's better to give than receive." Well, it's true.

The message of your music is more than just the music. It's a message of joy, love, and healing for the world to hear.

Conclusion

Now Do It!

"Knowledge is not power. It's only potential power. It only becomes power when we apply it and use it."

~ Jim Kwik

NOW THAT YOU have read about some key concepts of music, how to set goals, how to practice, how to deal with your fears and self-criticism, and how to communicate your music effectively, it's time for you to take action.

Before we talk about the next logical action step, I'd like to share one last story with you.

'Play pretty for the people'

I was about to go on one of my first tours playing with my jazz trio. I had studied with Mike for many years, and after being a struggling student and then a young pro, it was as if I had finally graduated. I was hitting the road the same way all the jazz greats did. This was a real feeling of triumph. *I did it.*

I felt the urge to thank Mike personally the night before my plane took off. He'd not only seen me through my musical growth starting as a teenager, but also helped me navigate numerous personal ups and downs, self-doubt, and obstacles along the way.

Through his inner-game guidance, I booked a tour and was packed and ready to fly to Europe for the first time as a bandleader.

As I was leaving his apartment and rang for the elevator, he offered me the parting words: "Go play pretty for the people."

These words went directly into my heart like a lightning bolt. They carried an unbelievable amount of meaning for me because the depth of our musical and personal story was summed up so simply in them. Those five words underlined thousands of hours together in a way only we could understand.

Essentially he was instructing me to use all the hard-earned knowledge and skill, which I'd paid for with blood, sweat, and tears, for one end; *to lift the hearts and souls of my audience.* Not to impress them, not to accrue fame, but to play beautifully and light their souls.

When a musician plays beautifully, it is an offering of love to the audience. Mike taught me to strive to "be as a hollow reed through which the Divine can pass through and communicate."

Fast-forward twelve years. As I was hunting for a title for my most recent CD release, this entire story flashed through my mind. My eyes welled up with tears. I knew that the title of the

CD had to be "Play Pretty for the People" because this sums up so much, so beautifully. It's a belief I hold dearly.

With this in mind, I am asking you to do the same. Go play pretty for the people. Allow this goal to guide and inspire you as you learn and practice.

Figuring out your next musical action step

Inspiration may be the wind beneath your wings, but you'll need to take concrete action steps to achieve your goals.

Before you decide what action step you'll take, let's recap what you've learned:

- In Chapter One you learned that **your musical intuition is perfect**. All your music must pass the gut test. This sense of musical perfection is not ego—it's more akin to the truth—*your* truth.

- In Chapter Two you learned to **stay tuned to that which lights your soul up musically**. It's different for everyone, but it's essential that you stay honest to who you are.

- In Chapter Three you learned techniques to **visualize how you'd like your life and music to be.** Go wild and envision your dreams. The more vivid detail you create your vision with, the more your subconscious mind sees it, and will try to close the gap between where you are and where you want to be. The subconscious will work 24/7 to make your dream a reality.

- In Chapter Four you learned about **the importance of having a teacher,** the **three stages of musical growth,** and the **balance between feelings and knowledge**. Remember: professionals don't rely on feelings.

- In Chapter Five you learned there are **ten areas of musical study** divided into two groups: **what to play and how to play.** What to play includes harmony, melody, rhythm, counterpoint, and form. How to play includes touch, time, tone, technique, and taste.

- In Chapter Six you learned about the **four stages of learning**, looking for results versus **putting in the time**, the importance of **getting started easily** and having **a proper practice environment.**

- In Chapter Seven you learned **how to get out of a rut** and understand plateaus in learning. Progress is not a steady climb, but rather a rhythm of sudden leaps followed by plateaus (which seem like periods of nothing).

- In Chapter Eight you learned how to practice guitar effectively and **build an effective practice routine.**

- In Chapter Nine you learned some basics about how to **get out there to perform**, where to look for performance opportunities, and what environments might be best for you.

- In Chapter Ten you learned tactics for **dealing with nervousness, stage fright, and your inner critic.**

- In Chapter Eleven you learned techniques for effective musical communication and **making it easy for your audience to love and appreciate your music.**

Listen to the little voice within

What is your gut telling you about your next logical step? Or what is it that you know you've been avoiding?

As you've read through this book, I bet there's been a little voice in your mind, hinting at what you need to do next. What is that voice saying?

Perhaps it has been telling you to:

- Get a teacher
- Get some recording gear
- Get together with musicians to jam
- Listen to a new style of music
- Attend a music camp
- Set up a practice environment
- Block practice time into your schedule
- Make a music video to share online
- Book your first gig
- Or anything else

If you're not sure what your next step is, you can never go wrong by getting a teacher you trust and getting some feedback. A teacher can hold you accountable and correct small mistakes in real time, saving you tons of time in the end.

And remember this: once your teacher gives you an assignment, it can seem very un-sexy.

You may have glamorous visions of playing live onstage, yet a teacher may show you something as mundane and boring as left-hand position. It's only after you've passed through the learning that you'll realize your left-hand position *is* your guitar-playing onstage.

Allow for several lessons with a teacher. One lesson is dabbling and will bring you very little.

Now go give your music to the world

I'd like to thank you for spending this time with me reading this book. It has been my sincere joy to share these inner-game concepts and techniques with you.

In this day and age, when so much musical information and instruction is available online, I feel this world of inner-game wisdom has been missing.

Maybe you can learn scales on the internet, but the internet can't give you an understanding mentor who cares and will guide you along the path.

You were attracted to this book because you have a burning desire to learn and improve, and you have a musical message that needs to be heard.

You also knew there is an inner game of fingerstyle guitar that goes far beyond chord shapes and fingerpicking patterns.

So go ahead... visualize your delicious musical future. Take one, small, action step in that direction. Just get started, and watch what happens.

Your music is in you and wants to get out. Give it the love and attention it deserves.

Your audience is out there, waiting for your beautiful music to enter their hearts and lives. Don't leave them waiting. They need you more than you know.

Recommended Reading

Ask and It Is Given, by Esther and Jerry Hicks

Atomic Habits, by James Clear

Breaking the Habit of Being Yourself, by Dr. Joe Dispenza

Deep Work, by Cal Newport

Eat That Frog, by Brian Tracy

How to Fail at Almost Everything and Still Win Big, by Scott Adams

Letting Go, by Dr. David Hawkins

Mastery, by Robert Greene

Mastery: The Keys to Success and Long-Term Fulfillment, by George Leonard

Power vs. Force, by Dr. David Hawkins

Success Is for You, by Dr. David Hawkins

The Abundance Book, by Lester Levenson and Larry Crane

The Contrapuntal Harmonic Technique of the 18th Century, by Allen Irvine McHose

The Ego Is the Enemy, by Ryan Holiday

The Obstacle Is the Way, by Ryan Holiday

The One Thing, by Gary Keller and Jay Papasan

The Purple Cow, by Seth Godin

The Study of Counterpoint (Gradus ad Parnassum), by Johann Joseph Fux

The Success Principles, by Jack Canfield

The Ultimate Truth, by Lester Levenson and Larry Crane

The War of Art, by Stephen Pressfield

Theory and Musicianship for the Creative Jazz Improviser, by Mike Longo

Thinking Fast, Thinking Slow, by Daniel Kahneman

Tribes, by Seth Godin

Turning Pro, by Stephen Pressfield

Win the Crowd, by Steve Cohen

Zen in the Art of Archery, by Eugen Herrigel

Zen Mind, Beginner's Mind, by Shunryu Suzuki

Acknowledgements

Writing this book has been a deeply emotional and profound experience. It's tapped a wellspring of gratitude within me as I review my musical and life journey. I could not have done it without the following people.

To Mike Longo, may you rest in peace. Thank you for sharing your and Dizzy Gillepie's musical discoveries and insights with me, for teaching me the African mother rhythm, counterpoint, harmony, melody, and having me play in your big band. Thank you for playing piano on my first two CD's. Thanks for the spiritual and psychological guidance, music lessons, business coaching, encouragement, and countless hours you spent with me as I went through so many personal ups and downs. You were more than just a music teacher. You were a true mentor, a guiding light, a second father, and a best friend. I hope to pay forward what you have given me to the next generation of musicians. I am forever thankful.

Judith Frechinger, thank you for being my loving partner with a huge heart and perfect musical instinct. You support me unendingly and believe in me when I haven't had the strength to believe in myself. You hear my musical message with your heart, and therefore you really know who I am. You accept me as I am and always tell me the truth, which is sometimes uncomfortable but always good. I love you bigger than the sky.

To my Dad, Phil Rafferty. Thank you for giving me my first contact with music. You played your Martin D-28 guitar for me as soon as I was born, which hardwired me with love for the instrument. I will never forget the smell of the wood, the incredible sound, the plush blue velvet inside of the case, and how fun it was to open and close the clips of the case when I was little. Because of your love for guitar and singing, my lifelong love affair with the guitar and music started. You were the first dude I ever jammed with. I love you, Dad.

To my Mom, Josie Rafferty, may you rest in peace. You supported me and my music lovingly and always made sure I had music lessons and instruments growing up. You introduced me to your old Beatles records, and listening to them with you on weekends inspired me to no end. You supported my guitar studies and career, and never thought twice about it. Your own artistic excellence in crochet and watercolor painting was an example of true handcraft, which made me also want to use my hands for art, just like you did. I love you, Mom.

Tommy Emmanuel, thank you for showing up in my life and giving me the unexpected inspiration to play solo fingerstyle guitar. I separate my life into two phases: before T.E. and after T.E. You showed me that a single person with an acoustic guitar could bring a listener to tears, or be a thundering one-man rock band. Discovering you and your music was a life changer. Your artistic excellence is a gift to guitarists and listeners all over the world. You raised the bar for all of us, and will forever be one of the greats. Thank you, Tommy.

Bob Cranshaw, may you rest in peace. Thank you for your

world-class bass playing on my second CD, "Blood Sweat and Bebop" in 1997. I have listened to your bass work on that CD thousands of times, and my jaw still hits the floor every time I hear your bass lines, your tone, and your groove. You have wholly informed the sound I try to achieve on guitar and remain one of my biggest musical influences.

Jimmy 'Preacher' Robins, may you rest in peace. Thank you for all the late nights and early mornings in Harlem. Making music with you and your Hammond B3 organ was unforgettable. You'd come to life after your second shot glass of Johnny Walker Red, and then proceed to threaten people with an eight-inch carving knife, and start fistfights. Between sets, you'd take me for late-night drives up and down Lenox Avenue in your white Cadillac. You were the real thing, sometimes too real. You put a musical fire under me that made me play the blues and groove with an intensity I didn't know I had. When I'm on stage now, I see your intense stare in my mind's eye, egging me on to dig deep within myself and play more soulfully and more grooving. You taught me "not to just toot my horn, but to do a complete show!"

Paul Beaudry, thank you for your close friendship, the invitation to be your duo partner on your "New Tomorrows" CD project, your perfectly swinging and tasty bass playing, and for the accountability partnership we have had for the past thirteen years. It all started with our weekly Wednesday 10 am coffee at Startbucks. You have helped me think things through, plan new projects, improve my health, and stay in the game. Thank you, my man.

John-Christian Urich aka "Cooly-C"... thank you for being my lifelong best friend and one of the finest drummers and songwriters I know. From the time we played in bands as teenagers, your insane energy, impeccable groove, wild sense of humor, and musical honesty have influenced me beyond words. Your disciplined work ethic and follow-through are exemplary. Wanna know a secret? I'm your biggest fan.

Henry Olsen, thank you for the friendship and much-needed daily phone calls which keep me inspired and sane. You always listen, provide encouragement, empathy, and accountability partnership. Let's keep rockin' it and not lose our minds with all the crazy online aspect of what we do!

Robert Fertitta, thank you for teaching me music theory in my college years at S.U.N.Y. Purchase. Your classes were an inspiration. You played piano beautifully and brilliantly for us, and your unending love for the music of the great composers always shone like rays of the sun from you. I will never forget when we sang J.S. Bach's Fugue in E major from WTC Book II in solfege class as an ensemble. That was a life-changing experience for me and informed my music profoundly.

Woody Mann, thank you for teaching me guitar at age six. My weekly lessons with you were highlights of my childhood. From the start, you made music fun and soulful. You were my favorite superhero at the time.

Dennis Cinelli and Pat O'Brien, may you both rest in peace. Thank you both for teaching me classical guitar. Your patient lessons lifted me from being just a talented kid to being a competent musician. I would not be where I am today without having studied with you both.

Jessi Rita Hoffman, thank you for editing this book so that my message comes through to my readers with clarity. You make a confused guitar picker like me actually seem like I know what I am talking about. Fooled 'em again!

A Message from the Author

I started learning guitar at age six from fingerstyle-blues-guitar legend Woody Mann, then studied classical guitar as a teenager. During college I began an intense musical apprenticeship with jazz pianist, composer, and arranger Mike Longo (formerly with Dizzy Gillespie). My twenty-year apprenticeship with Mike brought me priceless musical knowledge and profound emotional, psychological, and spiritual insights.

In 2007, fingerstyle guitar became my primary focus, and since then I've been extremely fortunate. My YouTube videos have gathered over twenty-million views, my CD "I Remember Michael" was hailed as one of the top ten CD's of 2010 by *Jazziz Magazine*, and I've gotten to play on stages every year for thousands of people in the U.S.A., Germany, Austria, Italy, Switzerland, Spain, France, Singapore, Thailand, Kazakhstan, Russia, Bermuda, England, Scotland, Estonia, Finland, Czech Republic, Belgium, Serbia, and other places.

I'm not only passionate about touring and performing, but also about teaching fellow guitarists how to achieve their full artistic, human, and spiritual potential through music.

That's why I wrote this book. I wanted to inspire you to carry on with your guitar journey and to master the inner challenges you may be facing. I hope what you've read here has helped you to overcome any self-doubt or limiting beliefs you may have harbored, so you can share your beautiful music with the world.

If you need any help or support, or just want to reach out and say hi, you can email me at adam@adamrafferty.com. I answer all emails personally.

You can also find me on the web at:

- http://adamrafferty.com

- http://studywithadam.com

- http://fingerstyleguitarhangout.com

Groove on! And also, *read* on, because at in the next few pages you'll find a listing of all my products and services, including an invitation to study with me personally.

Whenever you buy one of my books, I donate 5% of the profits to the Animal Welfare Institute https://awionline.org/. Since 1951, the institute has dedicated itself to reducing animal suffering caused by people. The AWI seeks to:

- Abolish factory farms and support high-welfare family farms

- Encourage the development of alternatives to experimentation on live animals

- End the use of steel-jaw leg-hold traps and reform other brutal methods of capturing and killing wildlife

- Preserve species threatened with extinction

- Protect companion animals from cruelty and violence

- Prevent injury and death of animals caused by harsh transport conditions

Since these helpless critters can't speak, I thank you on their behalf. Your purchase of this book has helped to spread a ray of love in the world.

Adam

Want to Learn More?

It's my joy to help you become a better guitar player, musician, and all-around happy and successful person.

If you'd like to get more instruction from me, there are several formats available.

- Free guitar lessons at http://adamrafferty.com
- On-demand video downloads and DVD's
- Personal online coaching at http://studywithadam.com
- Live concerts, workshops, and speaking engagements

Free Guitar Lessons

At http://adamrafferty.com/lessons you can get some great guitar-lesson downloads for free, so it's a good place to start.

These lessons are for the intermediate-level guitar player. If you can already play some chords, these lessons should be a good fit. Be warned, though: they will challenge you!

Some song lessons like "Vitamin E Blues" and "Silent Night" have full video instruction in addition to the PDF guitar tablatures, so you can follow my hands, note for note.

There are also technique lessons, special fingerings for scales, arpeggios, recording tips and more… all free!

Visit http://adamrafferty.com/lessons

On-Demand Videos and DVD Courses

These are more in-depth and advanced than the free goodies.

Learn how to play many of my well-known solo fingerstyle-guitar arrangements, with step-by-step videos, shown note for note. These are available via on-demand online video and DVD. (In the future, they may be available via download only, as DVD's are becoming unpopular and impractical.)

- **How to Play the Music of Stevie Wonder Vol. 1 for Solo Fingerstyle Guitar** (Full sheet music, tabs, and step-by-step video instruction for the Stevie Wonder classics "Superstition," "Overjoyed," "I Wish," and "Sir Duke")

- **How to Play the Music of Stevie Wonder Vol. 2 for Solo Fingerstyle Guitar** (Full sheet music, tabs, and step-by-step video instruction for the Stevie Wonder classics "Isn't She Lovely," "You Are the Sunshine of My Life," "Higher Ground," and "My Cherie Amour")

- **How to Play the Music of the Jackson Five for Solo Fingerstyle Guitar** (Full sheet music, tabs, and step-by-step video instruction for the Jackson Five classics "ABC," "I Want You Back," "I'll Be There," and "Never Can Say Goodbye")

- **Fingerstyle-Guitar Favorites** (Full sheet music, tabs,

and step-by-step video instruction for four of my favorite original songs "The Hippie Dance," "Rolling With the Ashes," "Jill's Song," and "Harlem")

- **How to Solo Over II-V-I Changes for Jazz Guitar** (a jazz guitar instructional DVD showing you how to improvise melodic lines that weave through chord changes)

For more information on these titles,
visit http://adamrafferty.com/store

Personal Guitar Coaching

Even if we are thousands of miles apart, you can now get custom-tailored, one-on-one coaching from me. This is my members-only, online guitar academy, called "Study with Adam." Beginners are as welcome as musicians whose skills are intermediate or advanced. I invite you to sign up for a **free, fourteen-day trial** at

http://studywithadam.com

This coaching has two parts:

The Watch-and-Play Video Library

- Here you'll find full-length, step-by-step video lessons for many of my popular fingerstyle-guitar arrangements, plus theory courses, harmony, arranging, and more. Each lesson includes a PDF help file so you can print material out for the music stand in your practice room.

- The library includes over a hundred hours of lessons. I add a few mega-lessons every year, so this resource is always expanding. These lessons are not currently available anywhere else for purchase.

Personal Video Feedback

- When you are ready, you can submit a video of yourself playing guitar, and I will respond with a personal video reply, precisely tailored to you and where you are at, just as if we were together doing a lesson in person. (The limit for this feature is one video upload per month.)

- You may choose to keep your uploads private, but many of my students make them public so the entire *Study with Adam* community can see them. (Undoing the privacy setting makes your upload visible only to SWA members, not to the general public.)

- Shared lesson videos serve as master-classes for all the students in our community to watch and learn from. Many students watch all the exchanges as part of their monthly training. The community engagement is encouraging, energizing, and keeps you in the game and practicing when motivation wanes.

In-Person Concerts, Live Guitar Workshops, and Speaking Engagements

I love traveling, seeing the world, making new friends, and bringing my music to new places when I am on tour. In fact, I'd love to meet *you*!

I'm available for concert bookings and live guitar workshops. Often these two go hand-in-hand. Maybe a concert at night and a workshop the day following.

I'm also available for speaking engagements. Many of the ideas presented in this book cross over into other disciplines. It's always a pleasure to speak to groups in other fields of study about creativity, self-discipline, goal setting, the learning process, and more.

Feel free to send an email to
office@adamrafferty.com for more information.

As a thank you for purchasing this book, I'd like to offer you some free online resources, which you can access by visiting or clicking on the link below.

Enjoy this good stuff!

http://adamrafferty.com/inner-game-book-free-gift

Made in the USA
Coppell, TX
19 January 2023

11334022R00132